Tackling Computer Projects

in Access with Visual Basic for Applications

3rd edition

P.M.Heathcote

B.Sc.(Hons), M.Sc.

Updated for Access 2000 by:

F.R.Heathcote

Payne-Gallway Publishers Ltd
78 Christchurch Street
Ipswich
IP4 2DE
Tel: 01473-251097 Fax: 01473 232758
E-mail: info@payne-gallway.co.uk   Web site: http//www.payne-gallway.co.uk

2000

Acknowledgements

I would like to thank Helen Williams for reading the manuscript for the second edition and making valuable comments and suggestions which I have incorporated into the text. Grateful thanks go to my daughter Flora who did much of the original work of developing the application described in this book for a local business, and who has updated the book to Access 2000 for the 3rd edition.

A CIP catalogue entry for this book is available from the British Library

ISBN 1 903112 22 2

Copyright PM Heathcote © 2000

First edition 1992. Reprinted 1993, 1996
Second edition 1997. Reprinted 1998, 1999
Third edition 2000. Reprinted 2001, 2002

Printed in Great Britain by
W M Print Ltd
45-47 Frederick Street
Walsall, West Midlands

Foreword

Pat Heathcote's books provide many students, their lecturers and teachers with clear, concise information on a wide range of computing topics. Students find her books easy to use for initial learning and as a revision aid.

'Tackling Computer Projects' has become a standard text for students providing an indispensable guide to the development of their project work. The book gives an insight into the tasks and structure required to develop a successful Computing or Information Technology project at any level from GNVQ Advanced, GCE Advanced Level to Higher National Diploma and beyond.

The third edition has been revised to incorporate new examination board requirements for the 2000 specifications and the advances in software available to students. Once again, this book is very easy to read and would be an invaluable guide to anyone developing a Computing or Information Technology project. As many students now choose to use MS Access and Visual Basic as their software development tools, chapters four to nine will be particularly helpful in aiding their production of a really professional computerised system.

Students following the advice and guidance provided in this book should be able to produce a project report that is worthy of a good grade and also develop a real, useable software solution. Any project that satisfies these criteria brings the dual satisfaction of a good academic grade together with a job well done.

Helen Williams
Principal Moderator and Examiner
February 2000

iii

Preface to the third edition

Aim

The aim of this book is to provide students with a comprehensive and practical guide on how to tackle a computing project for an Advanced Level or GNVQ Computing or Information Technology course. It will also be useful to students doing a project for a GCSE or Higher National computing course, since the principles remain the same at any level.

Need

Practical computing projects may comprise 20% or 33% of the final mark on an Advanced Level Computing or Information Technology course. Students very often find it difficult to think of a suitable idea for a computing project, and having come up with an idea, find the analysis and design stages extremely difficult to get started on. This is very understandable because in the practice assignments and projects set in the early part of their course, the students are normally given tasks to complete for which the analysis and design has already been done. Their limited experience of the advanced features of the various packages available makes it hard for them to know what can be achieved, and to evaluate different methods of solution.

The student therefore needs to be given at this point:

- Plenty of ideas for possible projects to spur his/her imagination, with some advice on what constitutes a suitable project
- A complete specimen project together with advice on how each stage (analysis, design, etc.) is tackled.

Approach

This book is suitable for students either on a taught course or studying independently, as it can be used with no additional help from a lecturer. Answers to all questions are given in the text.

Part 1 of the book follows through all the steps involved in writing a computer project, from the initial idea right through to the final documentation, with a specimen project being used to illustrate the various stages of development and implementation. Quick answer questions within the chapters encourage students to think about the material covered and to develop the skills needed for their own projects. MS Access has been used as the software development tool, and step-by-step instructions on how to complete each step are provided for Access 2000, Access 7 for Windows 95 and Access 2 (used with Windows 3.1).

Part 2 contains the prototype project, together with comments and grades that would be achieved for each section if it were submitted to the AQA as an A Level project. Other boards have similar grading criteria.

Part 3 shows the final project developed from the prototype to a finished solution satisfying all the objectives set out by the user. Comments and grades are once again included.

Lecturers' supplement

The prototype and final versions in Access 2, Access 7 and Access 2000 (i.e. six versions of the application) are available free to lecturers from our web site www.payne-gallway.co.uk

Contents

Foreword   iii
Preface   iv

		Pages	
		From	*To*
Part 1	Choosing a project	1 – 4	1 – 10
	Analysis	1 – 11	1 – 20
	Design	1 – 21	1 – 30
	Prototyping	1 – 31	1 – 50
	Developing the prototype	1– 50	1 – 65
	Optimising data entry	1 –66	1 – 86
	Helping the user to look up information	1 – 87	1 – 94
	Concentrating on output	1 – 95	1 – 100
	Debugging aids	1 – 101	1 – 104
	Testing	1 – 105	1 – 107
	The report	1 – 108	1 – 112
Part 2	Specimen Project 1 – Prototype		
	A.B.Frames Customer Database		
	Analysis	2 – 4	2 – 7
	Design	2 – 8	2 – 13
	Testing	2 – 14	2 – 16
	System maintenance	2 – 17	2 – 20
	User documentation	2 – 21	2 – 21
	Appraisal	2 – 21	2 – 23
Part 3	Specimen Project 2 – Final version		
	A.B.Frames Customer Database		
	Analysis	3 – 4	3 – 9
	Design	3 – 10	3 – 20
	Testing	3 – 21	3 – 28
	System maintenance	3 – 29	3 – 32
	User documentation	3 – 33	3 – 33
	Appraisal	3 – 33	3 – 36
	User manual	3 – 37	3 – 48
	Appendix 1 – Test data	3 – 49	3 – 53
	Appendix 2 – Module listings	3 – 54	3 – 60
	Index to Part 1		

Part 1

How to approach each stage of a project

Part 1 takes you through all the stages involved in choosing and completing a successful computer project. Chapter by chapter, you will learn techniques to help develop a system for a real end-user through the prototype stage to the finished product.

Table of Contents

Chapter 1 – Choosing a Project ...4
Requirements for a computer project 4
Choice of hardware and software 4
The choice of project 5
Choosing your own project 5
Drawing up a schedule or timetable 6
A sample schedule 6
Ideas for computer projects 6
Database and file-based projects 6
Computer-aided learning packages 8
Spreadsheet projects 8
Expert systems 9
Computer-aided design 10
Unsuitable topics 10
Specimen project described in this book 10

Chapter 2 – Analysis 11
The investigation 11
SPECIMEN PROJECT –
   A. B. FRAMES LTD 11
Preparing for an interview 12
Results of the interview 13
Adding in more detail 15
Detailed analysis 15
Comments on this project 16
Ascertaining the objectives 17
General objectives for a system 17
Drawing a data flow diagram 18
Consideration of possible solutions 19
Proposed solution 19
Writing up the analysis 19
Before you continue any further 20

Chapter 3 – Design 21
Take time over design 21
Overall system design 21
Producing a conceptual model 21
Input content, format and validation 22
Naming conventions 23
Data validation 25
Checklist of facts to record about each
   data item 25
Output 25
The user interface 25
Module design and specification 28
Security and backup 28
Designing a test strategy 28

Chapter 4 – Prototyping 31
Why prototype? 31
Building a prototype for the specimen
   project 31
Creating a new database 32
Creating the database tables 32
Defining relationships between tables 35
Creating a form for entering Customer details . 35
Creating a form for entering Job details 37
Testing the data entry forms 42
Creating and saving queries to select different
   categories of customer 43
Creating a report listing all business
   customers 43
Creating mailing labels for all business
   customers 44
Creating a mail merge letter 45
Providing the user with instructions for
   performing a mail merge 47
Creating the menu system 47
Finishing off the prototype 49
The next step 49

Chapter 5 – Developing the
   Prototype 50
Using the prototype as a design tool 50
Creating a combo box to find records 51
Programming with macros 54
Programming in Visual Basic or
   Access Basic (Access 2) 57
Handling multiple matching records 59
Using the online Help in Access 2000 &
   Access 7 62
Using the online Help in Access 2 64

Chapter 6 – Optimising Data
   Entry 66
Providing data entry shortcuts 66
Automatically incrementing the CustomerID .. 66
Customising the form's tab order 69
Setting default values in controls 71
Referring to database objects 72
Entering details of a new job 73
Customising the frmJobSheet form 77
Automatic calculations 81
Smartening up the fsubItem Subform 82

Chapter 7 – Helping the User to Look Up Information 87

Adding the facility to look up jobs 87
Using global variables 88
Putting finishing touches to data entry forms... 94

Chapter 8 – Concentrating on Output 95

Querying the database 95
Performing the mail merge 97
Making the Main Menu load automatically 99
Adding a password 99

Chapter 9 – Debugging Aids 101

Types of error 101
Using the Immediate window (called
Debug window in Access 7) 101
Setting a breakpoint to stop running code 102
Stepping through code line by line 103
Stepping over procedures 103
Using a message box to display variables 104

Chapter 10 – Testing 105

Testing objectives 105
Designing a test plan 105
Steps in software testing 106
Drawing up a test plan 106
Selecting tests for the test plan 107
Presenting the test results 107

Chapter 11 – The Report 108

Introduction 108
Should the documentation be
wordprocessed? 108
Wordprocessing skills 109
How long should the documentation be? 109
Putting it all together 109
The title page 110
Table of contents 110
Analysis 110
Design 110
Testing 110
System maintenance 111
User manual 111
Appraisal 112

Chapter 1 – Choosing a Project

Objectives

By the end of this chapter you should:

understand what constitutes a suitable project;

understand the constraints on the choice of hardware and software;

know how to go about choosing your own project;

know how to work out a schedule to meet the project deadline;

have looked at summaries of several past projects of different types.

Requirements for a computer project

Generally, when a project forms part of a computing course, you will be expected to produce a **complete, well-documented system**. You have to demonstrate that you can solve an information processing problem using the most appropriate means available. Projects should be selected which allow you to demonstrate skills of practical application and problem solving, as well as the techniques of documentation and system testing. Note that for the AQA 'A' Level Computing exam although it is envisaged that you will develop a complete working solution, *the project report need only contain carefully selected samples of evidence in order to demonstrate each skill.*

You are more likely to develop a successful project if you can find a real user with a real problem to be solved. Otherwise the project turns into a textbook exercise with invented problems and unrealistic solutions.

Choice of hardware and software

If you are developing a project for a real user, you may be asked to produce software that will run on the equipment they already own, for example a PC or Apple Macintosh. This may be impossible if you do not have access to the same hardware or software at your college, school, home or office. If this is an exam project rather than something you are doing for payment, you would be well advised to use the hardware and software that you have easy access to, even if the system is never actually implemented for the user. Most users understand the constraints that you are working under and will still be happy to explain their current system and what the requirements of a new system would be. There is always the possibility that you could convert it at a later date if they really want it!

You may not have much choice of hardware, and this book assumes that you will have access only to a standalone or networked PC with a standard keyboard input and a printer of some kind.

There may be a wide range of software to choose from. If you want to write a complete database application, software such as MS Access may be a good option. A computer-aided design system may be easier to program in 'C'. If you are thinking of computerising the accounts of a small business, a specialised accounting package may be your best choice. But ultimately, you will have to choose from the software that you or your college or school have, even if the project could be done better or faster another way.

The choice of project

Choosing a project is the first hurdle. It needs to be sufficiently meaty to enable you to gain the maximum possible marks, but not so ambitious that you cannot get it finished in the time available.   About 20% of the marks may be awarded for 'Analysis of requirements', which will include finding out how the current system works and what the inputs and outputs are, as well as what the user would like the new system to do. Obviously, it is going to be much easier to get these marks if you have a real user with a real problem to be solved, or a real application which would benefit from computerisation.

By contrast, if for example you choose to create a new computer game, it may be difficult or impossible to fulfil the criteria set by your Examination Board. For example, the AQA specifies that 'candidates should investigate a *real* problem associated with a user whose realistic needs should be taken into account when designing the solution.'

Typically, an A Level Computing or Information Technology candidate is expected to:

a) analyse a real and realistic problem, identify the requirements of a potential user and identify the parts which are appropriate for a computer solution;

b) determine the requirements for a computer solution, specify possible solutions and select an appropriate one;

c) select and apply appropriate techniques and principles to develop algorithms for the solution of problems;

d) implement algorithms to produce a documented and tested system using, as appropriate, existing or purpose-designed software, and appropriate hardware.

All Boards have somewhat similar standards. You should check the specification for your own Examining Board to make sure your choice of project is appropriate.

Choosing your own project

The most important things to remember when you choose your project are:

♦ Choose something that interests you – after all, you are going to spend the next several months on it.   If you are a member of a football club or cricket club, or have a part-time job in a restaurant, shoe shop or sports centre, for example, observe or ask how things are done at present.   Organisations such as clubs or societies involve administrative functions which could often benefit from some form of computerisation.

♦ Many ideas which at first seem lacking in scope can be turned into very good projects with a little imagination. Careful work on the user interface, file design and output goes a long way. But be realistic – is it really worth using a computer to keep records of fifteen people in the badminton club who each pay an annual subscription of £5.00?

♦ Whatever your strengths and weaknesses in computing, as soon as you start work on your project you will probably realise you don't know how to tackle part of it. Perhaps you don't know enough about file design, or you would like to use the function keys in a program but don't know how. You may find some of the answers in this book, but very likely you will have to do extra research on your own. Try the library first, and if that has nothing, splash out and buy a good book on Visual Basic, Delphi or Access, or whatever package you intend to use.

♦ If the thought of 'data processing' and updating files bores you, consider other areas of your specification such as compiler-writing, expert systems, simulation, graphics or process control. Again, you will have to do your own research and this will probably mean both time and money, but it could be worth it. Check the requirements of your specification first; an Information Technology specification may require you to use generic applications software rather than using a general-purpose programming language.

Drawing up a schedule or timetable

Obviously your schedule will depend on the length of time you have available to complete the project. On a two-year 'A' level course, you should probably start thinking of ideas in the summer term of your first year, and start on the analysis in the holidays or immediately you return in September. Spend time doing careful design work for the whole project before you start programming in the second half of the term.

Testing the system and writing up the documentation can take as long as writing the programs, so be sure to leave enough time for this before the deadline. Once you have done the initial design work you can draw up a detailed schedule of programs or forms, reports etc. to be designed, coded and tested.

A sample schedule

task	start date	finish date (estimated)
Analysis	Sep 5	Sep 30
Design	Oct 1	Oct 14
Prototype	Oct 15	Nov 14
Further Design	Nov 15	Nov 30
Programming	Dec 1	Jan 31
System testing	Feb 1	Feb 20
User Evaluation	Feb 21	Mar 7
Documentation	Mar 1	Mar 20
Hand in:		Mar 30

Ideas for computer projects

Projects can be put roughly into 'categories', and a number of project summaries from various categories are given below.

Database and file-based projects

Many good projects involve file handling of some sort. Nearly all these projects will involve storing information on a master file or database, querying and updating it. This in itself is not enough to form a project – ask yourself what the POINT of the system is. There is no point putting data INTO a system if you don't get anything OUT of it, so concentrate on what the output will be. Generally speaking a reasonably substantial project will involve more than one file – perhaps a file of transactions as well as a master file, or two master files linked in some way. A complete database will almost certainly involve several related tables.

1. **Newsagent's Database**

    Summary: The main objectives of this system are:

    to make delivery orders easier to implement;

    to allow paper price changes to be made quickly and easily;

    to allow data retrieval for a specific customer;

    to print a daily sheet for each paperboy specifying which papers are to be delivered to each customer;

    to make paper orders to suppliers more accurate by calculating exactly the number of papers needed;

    to make a billing system that is both itemised and clear.

    Comment: This is an ambitious project which could be made more manageable by omitting the billing side, while making provision for this to be programmed at a later date. The newsagent's requirements need careful analysis; for example, how are customers' holidays recorded, when no papers are required? The current method of recording data needs to be looked at and suitable report formats agreed with the prospective user. This is a good project for someone with experience as a paperboy/girl or who has worked in a newsagent's shop.

2. **Dressmaking Service Job Control**

    Summary: The project is designed to assist in the smooth running of a dress-making and clothes alteration business. Personal details on all customers (name, address, measurements, past orders etc.) are to be kept on a computerised file, and another file of 'jobs in progress' is also stored, giving details of date received, costs, hours worked and so on for costing purposes. When the job is completed an invoice is printed and the job details moved to the 'History file', linked to the correct customer.

    Comment: This project can involve some complex data structures and file handling, using for example a linked list to hold the file of past jobs linked to customer. Equally, it could be implemented using a database package such as Microsoft Access. The low volume of data may make it hard to justify the use of a computer but the system could be looked upon as a prototype for a much larger operation.

3. **Theatre Booking System**

    Summary: The aim of this system is to handle bookings for plays (either for an amateur Dramatic Society or a local theatre), keeping a database of plays, customers and seats booked. Tickets need to be printed, and management reports may be required showing the attendance for different plays or seasons. Letters may be mailed to selected customers if bookings are slow for a particular show.

    Comment: It is absolutely essential to have a real user here, to get a clear set of objectives rather than making up your own. If you have worked in a theatre booking office or can spend a day observing and asking questions, this could make an interesting project. The main difficulty with any type of booking system is deciding how to display the available seats (or tennis courts, cottages, etc).

4.   **School Administration**

Summary: There may well be some parts of your school or College administration that could benefit from computerisation. For example, students enrolled in the A Level programme at XXX College have their name, address and course code held on the central college database. However, the administrator of the A Level programme needs more information than is provided by the College database, such as which subjects they are taking and who their personal tutors are. Class lists can then be prepared for the subject tutors, and grades can be recorded when available so that subject teachers can be informed.

Comment: Once again, a real user is required to explain what would be needed from a new computerised system and exactly what output is required.

Computer-aided learning packages

5.   **Interactive History for Year 10**

Summary: This project uses an authoring package called Authorware to create an interactive package for Year 10 History pupils. Animation, photographic images, questions and answers are used to capture a pupil's attention and interest and help him/her to remember essential facts.

Comment: This project requires a good understanding of the material to be taught, the characteristics of the learners, knowledge of how to design a lesson and skill in setting multiple choice type questions as well as mastery of the software. Analysis and design will be somewhat different from that required for a data-processing type of project, and you really need specialised advice before embarking on such a project.

6.   **Typing tutor for child with impaired vision**

Summary: This project is designed to help children with severely impaired vision to learn keyboard skills.

Comment: If the project is done by a student who has personal knowledge of a child with impaired vision and can therefore perform a real analysis of user needs, this can be developed into an interesting and useful project.

Spreadsheet projects

If you choose a project which involves a lot of calculations and tables of data, a spreadsheet may be a good tool with which to implement it. The project must use the advanced features of the package; for example, in Excel it is possible to use macros and Visual Basic code to build an application complete with menus, data entry forms, command buttons and so on.

7.   **Farm Produce Sales Recording System**

   Summary: A farmer growing organic vegetables runs a farm shop from which the produce is sold. The farm is registered with the Soil Association as being an organic producer, and as such has annual inspections. To comply with the Soil Association's criteria on inspection the farmer is required to keep detailed records of the amount of produce of each kind sold on every day the shop is open. The shop has a cash register which keeps a record of the amount of money taken for each of about 25 different types of vegetable and at the end of the day it prints out a report showing these figures. The spreadsheet system will use these figures as input data and convert the currency amounts to weights of produce sold, calculate weekly and annual totals and print the necessary reports.

   Comment: This is a good project for implementation using a spreadsheet because it involves a lot of data which can be held in tabular form, calculations which can easily be done in a spreadsheet, and regular data input which can be done in a special area set aside in the spreadsheet and then copied automatically to the calculation area.

8.   **Stock control for a Wine Merchants**

   Summary: A spreadsheet is used to keep a list of all stock and stock transactions. Stock reports and reorder reports can be printed out as required.

   Comments: Stock control could also be implemented for any small organisation with a limited amount of stock. You are not recommended to try and rewrite Tesco's stock control system! It is essential to have first-hand knowledge of the business whose stock control you are computerising, and of the problems and objectives to be tackled.

Expert systems

9.   **An Expert System Shell**

   Summary: An expert system is designed to make the task of passing on your expert knowledge to other people as easy as possible. The first step is to set up the 'knowledge base', consisting of the possible outcomes and the questions which need to be asked to determine which outcome is the correct one. For example, your knowledge base could consist of British birds, and the questions would be 'Does it have a red breast?', 'Does it have a yellow beak?', and so on. The expert system shell is the software that allows the expert to enter and store the knowledge, and the non-expert to get an answer to his query by replying to questions posed by the computer until it is able to make a decision. The objectives of this project, then, are to:

   have facilities for creating, editing and storing a knowledge base;

   be able to make decisions at least as accurately as a human expert;

   be able to make a decision even though it has not been given all the information;

   explain its decision to the user.

   Comment: This is a really interesting project for someone interested in Expert Systems. You would need to look at other Expert System shells such as Crystal or EASIE, do some research into how expert systems work, and then devise your own algorithm. This one used a system of allowing the user to give a 'weight' to each answer so that the outcome with the highest 'score' was selected. An expert system could also be implemented in Prolog.

Computer-aided design

10.   Computer-aided design package

Summary: The aim of the project is to create software which enables a user to enter drawings constructed from various geometrical shapes (lines, circles, rectangles, etc), and to move, size and rotate them.

Comment: This is a very complex project involving an understanding of the mathematics involved in rotating an object. It is best implemented with a 'GUI' (graphical user interface) using a mouse and symbols for line, circle, box, and so on.

Unsuitable topics

For both Computing and Information Technology projects, the system must involve a user inputting data of some kind, and obtaining output. The production of a document about some aspect of computing is therefore **not** suitable. For example:

♦   a project which consists of a comparative study of two wordprocessors;

♦   the production of a magazine using a desktop publishing system;

♦   a general description of how to use a particular spreadsheet or database package.

Specimen project described in this book

A single specimen project is used to illustrate all the stages involved in developing and documenting a project.

The project is implemented in MS Access. The use of a prototype to assist in the design of the final system is illustrated, and then used to demonstrate how to write Visual Basic modules to enhance and customise the final product to the user's requirements.

Part 2 illustrates how a project is typically tackled by a student who has not really got to grips with the standard required for a good grade. In Part 3, the same basic idea is developed to a much higher standard. Both projects are shown in a form suitable for handing in to an examiner, with comments that might be written by an internal assessor (e.g. your teacher) before sending the project off to the moderator.

AQA project guidelines have been quoted as an example of what examiners expect from student projects. However, BTEC, GNVQ and Advanced Level students studying for exams with other Examining Boards will find these guidelines are equally valid and relevant to their own projects. Naturally, you should study carefully the particular set of guidelines you have been given in addition to any advice in this book.

Summary

This chapter has covered:

♦   the requirements for a project;

♦   how to choose and schedule your project.

Chapter 2 – Analysis

Objectives

By the end of this chapter you will have considered the following points in the analysis of a system:

How to prepare for an interview with the end-user;

Points to cover in the interview;

The importance of ascertaining both quantitative and qualitative objectives;

The use of a data flow diagram;

Consideration of possible solutions;

Justification of chosen solution;

A possible framework for writing up the analysis.

The investigation

Once you have decided on your project topic, you must make a full investigation of the user's needs (the user may be a person you know, or know of, or you may have a **potential** user in mind if, for example, you are writing a game or an expert system shell). Be aware, though, that at Advanced Level, examination boards usually stress the need to actually find a **real** user and obtain **real user feedback**. Having a 'potential' user may reduce the project to one of a distinctly hypothetical nature, not able to satisfy any user at all – and scoring only modest marks.

At AS Level, it may be acceptable to investigate a problem which relates to a hypothetical situation with a *proposed* or envisaged user. For a 'minor project' in the first year of a modular course such as the AQA's Information Technology specification, your teacher may be able to set you a problem and act as the end-user. Nevertheless you are strongly advised to find your own end-user; if the same project is done by several students in a class, all of whom hand in a very similar implementation, you are unlikely to get credit for it even if most of the original ideas were yours.

The exercise of designing a questionnaire, or preparing a list of questions and holding interviews, should be regarded as an important part of the project; it is in practice quite impossible to guess what a real user would want from, say, a club membership system or sports hall booking system. A project based on a real user's problem will win hands down every time over one which tries to guess an imaginary user's requirements.

The analysis is concerned with finding out about the **current** system (if there is one), and what the **requirements** are for the new system.

SPECIMEN PROJECT – A. B. FRAMES LTD.

The specimen project shows how an analysis might proceed. You have established that A.B.Frames is a small family business run by Mr and Mrs Daniels which specialises in selling pictures and restoring and framing pictures, photographs, tapestries and so on. There is a possibility that part of their business could benefit from computerisation; specifically, to help them keep track of their customers and what particular artists, subjects etc. each customer is most interested in.

Typically, the owners of a business such as A.B.Frames may be members or friends of the family, or you may have been put in touch with them by your teacher.

Preparing for an interview

The first step in a project will usually be to plan an interview with the user. Make sure you have a list of questions prepared, and a notebook handy to write down the user's answers.

The involvement of a real user right from the start is a vital ingredient of a good project. You must show evidence of investigative competence in order to earn top marks in the analysis section.

You will find that preparing questions in advance of an interview focuses your attention on what information is needed, and the interview is less likely to end up as a vague chat about possibilities which still leaves a lot of unanswered questions.

If you have used a questionnaire, samples of the responses can be put into an Appendix, and a summary included in the analysis section of your report.

A checklist of points to cover in an interview might include the following:

1. objectives   exactly what is the new system designed to achieve?

2. input   what format does the input take? What input documents are currently used, and what are the data requirements?

3. output   what will be the output from the new system? Is hard copy required? How often? Is there some output from the current system or a similar system that you can look at?

4. processes   what is done, where, when and how? How are the objectives going to be fulfilled in the new system?

5. data   how much is there? Will the master file contain 50, 500 or 5000 records? How often does it change, or new records have to be added or deleted? Do these changes come in batches of several at a time, or in ones and twos?

6. exceptions   How are exceptions and errors handled?

7. security   Is security an issue? Should there be limited access to some or all parts of the new system?

8. problems   what are the drawbacks or problems with the current way of doing things?

9. constraints   are there any constraints on hardware, software, cost, time and so on?

10. suggested solutions   does the user have a particular solution in mind?

Quick Answer Questions

Suppose that you have decided to take on the task of computerising some or all of A.B.Frames' business.

1. Assume that you have the opportunity to interview the owner, Mrs Daniels. What questions will you ask her?

2. What documents could you ask to look at?

   (Answers overleaf)

QAQ Answers

1. You should go through the checklist of points to make sure they are covered. Obviously, the list of questions is going to be different for different situations, and you may already know quite a lot about the problem that you are going to solve with the aid of a computer, so don't stick slavishly to a formula. As you get answers, different questions will occur to you. Here is a possible list:

    ♦ Can you tell me how you think a computer may be able to help you in the running of your business?

    ♦ Can you show me how customer orders are currently recorded?

    ♦ What output would you hope to get from the current system?

    ♦ How many regular customers do you have?

    ♦ Do you already have a computer?

    ♦ Do you have any particular package in mind for this project?

2. Ask to see, for example:

    ♦ a sample order form

    ♦ any manual card index of customers

    ♦ a list of customers produced by the current system.

Results of the interview

The initial interview has elicited the following facts.

Each time a customer comes in to buy something or have a painting framed or restored, a job sheet is completed. The customer is given one copy, a second copy is sent to the workshop with the item to be framed or restored and a third copy is filed. An example is shown in Figure 2.1.

Frequently, a customer will come back several months later and ask, for example, for another tapestry to be framed 'using the same sort of frame as last time'. This means a lengthy search through hundreds of job sheets, and often the relevant one cannot be located.

The owners would also like some means of identifying which customers are interested in particular artists (e.g. dogs, landscapes, portraits), who are their best customers in terms of jobs or amount spent, which customers are business customers and so on, so that letters can be sent out inviting selected customers to special events, sales or exhibitions.

Mr and Mrs Daniels have recently purchased a PC and the MS Office suite, including MS Access. However they are finding it very hard to learn how to use Access and set up their own database, and have asked for a customised database application to be created. They would like to learn more about Access and Word themselves so that they could for example create a new letter to be sent to a selected set of customers.

A.B.Frames Limited

15 Castle Street, Ipswich IP8 5EW
Telephone (01473) 555322

Vat Reg No. 332 990477 32

Order No   *4842*

Date Required   *5th August*

Customer Name and Address

W Graham
12 Cranford Drive
Ipswich

Tel No.

Description of Work   *Old dog*

Frame   *193 Painted Blue*   Size   *14 x 17*

Conservation Mount [ ]   Colour   *Blush White*

Glass [ ]   Norm [ ]   N/R [ ]   Perspex [ ]

Back [ ]   Norm [ ]   S/U [ ]   Fitting [ ]

SPECIAL INSTRUCTIONS

Paid in Full

Price (inc VAT) £   Deposit Paid £

Figure 2.1: The Job Sheet

Adding in more detail

If the above couple of pages were to be handed in to the AQA as the Project Analysis, it would almost certainly fall into the second category of 'Some analysis but limited in perception and scope. It shows some evidence of investigation of a problem with limited scope resulting in a standard exercise with no external constraints. System objectives unclear or implicit. Little evidence of consideration of user requirements.' Mark: 4 out of 12.

To lift this analysis into the next category, you need to consider the problem in more detail. For instance, you could ask the following questions:

- what data needs to be held about each customer? (e.g. if the customer is a Business Customer, should we hold the name and address of their business?)
- what are the main objectives of the system?
- what data needs to be held about each job? Do we need to hold all the data on the current job sheets?
- is there ever more than one item per job?
- is the intention to enter jobs while the customer is actually at the shop counter, or will the jobs still be entered manually using the old job sheets, and then some of the information transferred later to the database?
- exactly what is the expected output from the system? Are any reports required?
- do we need to design and save queries to find various categories of customer such as 'all Business customers', or do the users want to be shown how to make queries themselves?
- how much of the Mail Merge operation should be automated?
- would it be a good idea to include an option to delete all customers who have been 'inactive' for say, the last three years?
- is a password system needed?
- should provision be made for automatically backing up the data?

Detailed analysis

More detailed enquiries about the proposed database revealed the following facts.

Input data

Data needs to be kept for both customers and jobs.

Customer data

The following data needs to be held for each customer:

  Name
  Address
  Business Customer ? (Y/N)
  Business name (if a business customer)
  Customer Interests: Framing/Sales/Restoration/Tapestry/Exhibition? (or any combination of these)

Job data

The current system of manually recording jobs is quite informal, and if a customer wants more than one picture framed, for example, two job sheets may be filled in with the same job number and notes made in the 'Special Instructions' field. **The new computerised system should allow for more than one item per job, for example a sale and a restoration**.

For each job, the following data must be stored:

Job Number

Job date

Customer name and address

Type of item: – sales, restoration or framing. (n.b. may be more than one different item)

Description

Type of frame (if framing item)

Artist name and subject matter (if sales)

Job value

Output

The following reports are required:

♦   a list of all business customers;

♦   a list of all customers whose total jobs exceed a given value;

♦   a list of all customers interested in, for example, a given artist, or given subject matter, or who fall into various categories such as 'Framing', 'Tapestry', 'Sales', 'Exhibition', 'Restoration'.

The owners would also like the ability to mail letters to selected customers.

Other requirements

An important requirement is that any customer information can be quickly located on screen, including details of all the jobs that customer has ordered in the past.

It is not intended to replace the current manual method of recording jobs. The jobs will still be recorded in the same way, and then entered into the database once a week. Possibly at a future date the manual system will be completely replaced, but the owners wish to proceed cautiously until they feel more confident with their PC and the Access software.

Comments on this project

This project has to be implemented in MS Access, because that is what the customer has requested. It offers plenty of scope, and can be tackled on a number of levels; the whole system could be implemented using 'wizards', but would it really meet the customer requirements?

In Advanced Level Computing, **examiners are unlikely to award the highest grades to a project which has not involved some programming of either macros or modules, or both.**

One approach is to use the 'wizards' at the Design stage to build a prototype of the final solution, which can be shown to the intended user who may then have some suggestions for other facilities they would like included. The prototype can then either be discarded or developed into the final solution.

It would be a good idea to include some evidence of user involvement at this stage, perhaps getting the user to 'sign off' the final design.

Figure 2.2: User involvement is essential and should be documented!

At AS Level, a well-developed and tested prototype may be perfectly adequate. The project is of much more limited scope and candidates are **not** expected to produce extensive segments of original code or extensive macro-programming.

Ascertaining the objectives

The objectives of the proposed new system need to be formally identified and stated. Turn to the second sample project to see how they have been written down. Where possible, you should include both **qualitative** and **quantitative** objectives.

An example of a qualitative objective is:

"It should be easy to locate a particular customer invoice".

An example of a quantitative objective is:

"It should be possible to locate any customer invoice in under 30 seconds".

The more clearly your objectives are stated, the easier it will be to evaluate your final solution with reference to the objectives.

General objectives for a system

The objectives for your own project will obviously be different from those for this project.

They may be, for example:

- ♦ to provide management information of some kind;
- ♦ to provide a better service to customers, members of a club, or anyone else affected by the new system;
- ♦ to save time and effort for the person who is currently performing the task manually;
- ♦ to perform some task better or more accurately than has previously been possible;

♦   to cut costs or save money in some way;

♦   to give enjoyment or entertainment to the user.

These general objectives need to be stated in specific, measurable terms for each individual project.

There are other objectives which are often given by students, but which are of dubious value. For example:

♦   *to create a user friendly system*

Yuk! This is a most overworked phrase. Granted, any system wants to be as easy to use as possible, but it is really not an end in itself. When stated as the first objective, it usually means that the student has not actually thought about what the real objectives are.

♦   *to enable me to learn more about object-oriented programming (or whatever)*

This needs to be a beneficial spin-off rather than the primary purpose of the project. If there isn't a real purpose, perhaps you should think of another project! The objectives will relate to the desired **output** of the system.

Analysis of the system is not something you can do in three-quarters of an hour. You must try to think yourself into the position of the 'user' and understand all the complexities of their task, if you are going to produce something really usable at the end of it all. You will probably keep coming back to your interview notes throughout the project, as problems crop up in the design and development stages. It is very important to keep notes of the preliminary investigation or interview to which you can refer. A summary of the main points of the interview can be included in the Analysis Section of the report, but bearing in mind the upper limit on the length of the report, a transcript is **not** required.

Drawing a data flow diagram

A data flow diagram is often a good way of summarising the sources and destinations of data, and the processing that takes place. It shows how data moves through a system and what data stores are used. It does not specify what type of data storage is used or how the data is stored.

A data flow diagram for the specimen project is shown in Part 3.

The following four symbols are used in data flow diagrams:

Entity – data source or data destination, such as people who generate data such as a customer order, or receive information such as an invoice

Process – an operation performed on the data. The two lines are optional; the top section of the box can be used to label the process, the middle to give a brief explanation, the bottom to say where the process takes place

Data store – such as a file held on disk or a batch of documents

Data flow – the arrow represents movement between entities, processes or data stores. The arrow should be labelled to describe what data is involved

Consideration of possible solutions

You need to consider carefully how the objectives will be best achieved. Should you use a package, or write a suite of programs? What programming language would be most suitable? Is that language available for you to use, or are you constrained by the software which you or the end-user has access to? Are there any constraints on hardware? Are you sure that a computerised solution is really the best one, or would it be preferable to improve the manual methods? (If so, think of another project!)

The most important person to consider is the end-user – in the case of the specimen project, the owner of the business. If she has a PC and wants to use Access, then your choices are pretty limited. Even so, you should at least write a justification of your chosen method of solution if this is requires by your specification. (Note that 'consideration of possible solutions' is not required by the AQA 'A' Level Computing specification.)

Proposed solution

Your proposed solution, describing the software and hardware you intend to use, should be stated and justified. You may be able to justify your choice on the grounds of what facilities a particular language or package has which will make your job easier, or the end product better in some way, or on cost grounds, or because your chosen language is the only one available in which you have sufficient expertise to undertake a programming task.

The trend in the past few years is for more and more students to choose to use a software package for their projects rather than writing a suite of programs. As the facilities offered by the various packages are generally quite easy to learn to use, and packages are becoming both cheaper and more powerful, this approach makes a good deal of sense and you should give it serious consideration. The implementation will probably be very much quicker, allowing you more time for thorough testing and documentation, both important aspects of a project. But remember that for an A Level project, you will be expected to do some programming of macros or modules even if you are using a software package.

Writing up the analysis

A possible framework for writing up the analysis is given below:

1. **Introduction**
   1.1 Background
   1.2 Initial user information
2. **Investigation**
   2.1 The current system (including summary of main points of interview if appropriate)
   2.2 Data flow diagram
   2.3 Problems with the current system

---

3.   Objectives of the new system

3.1   General objectives

3.2....3.n   Specific objectives

4.   Constraints

4.1   Hardware

4.2   Software

4.3   Time (including a well-defined schedule of activities)

4.4   User's knowledge of Information Technology

5.   Limitations of the new system

5.1   Areas which will not be included in computerisation

5.2   Areas considered for future computerisation

6.   Proposed solution

6.1   Appraisal of potential solutions

6.2   Justification of chosen solution

Of course, not every analysis will fit the model precisely! It is merely intended as a starting point from which you may diverge.

Before you continue any further

When you have written up the analysis, you should hand it in to your project supervisor (teacher or lecturer) to check that the proposals provide scope for sufficient range and depth to be a worthwhile AS or A Level project. If it isn't, it's better to face the truth sooner rather than later!

Your teacher should also be able to spot whether you have chosen a project that is too ambitious and is unlikely to be completed before the deadline. If that is the case, it should be possible to limit the project to a well-defined part of a larger system.

Summary

This chapter has covered the **analysis** of a system, which is concerned with how the **current** system works, and what the **requirements** of a new system would be. It involves:

♦   interviewing the user;

♦   establishing the objectives of the new system;

♦   identifying the input, output, data characteristics and processing methods used;

♦   finding out how errors and exceptions are handled;

♦   finding out what the constraints are if a new system is to be installed;

♦   appraising possible solutions and justifying your chosen solution;

♦   writing up the analysis;

♦   checking with your project supervisor that you are on the right lines thus far.

Chapter 3 – Design

Objectives

By the end of this chapter you will have covered the following points in the design of a system:

Overall system design;

Producing a conceptual model;

Drawing an entity-relationship diagram;

Analysis of data requirements;

Input content and format;

Data validation;

Output;

User interface design;

Charts showing overall systems design;

Program or module specification(s);

Security and backup;

Design of test strategy.

Take time over design

The Design stage is a crucial part of any project, since a poor design will almost certainly mean that the project will not be successfully implemented. Programming should not start until the design is completed. Someone once made the point that the design stage is often rushed in order to allow time at the end of the project to correct the mistakes that were caused by rushing the design stage...

Overall system design

In this section you should describe briefly the inputs, processing and outputs that make up the system. A **system outline chart** (see specimen project in Part 3) is a convenient way of showing these. A **systems flow chart** shows similar information but also shows the sequence of events.

Producing a conceptual model

From the statement of requirements, a conceptual data model can be produced. This will show the entities, attributes and relationships.

♦ An **entity** is a thing of interest to the business; for example customer, job.

♦ An **attribute** is a property or characteristic of an entity, such as customer name, address, job number.

- ♦ A **relationship** is a link or association between entities. For example there is a one-to-many relationship between customer and job.

The entities in the A.B. Frames application are CUSTOMER, JOB, and ITEM. You should show the relationships between the entities by drawing an **entity-relationship diagram**:

Figure 3.1: Entity-Relationship diagram

Input content, format and validation

Once you have produced a data model like the one above, you can start to design the structure of the database. Make sure the tables are correctly structured from your entity-relationship diagram, and then write down the attributes in each table, identify the primary key, and decide on any validations and default values that can be attached to any field.

The tables for A.B. Frames are defined as follows:

CUSTOMER   (Table name: **tblCustomer**)

Attribute Name	Data Type	Max Length	Default value	Description/ Validation
CustomerID*	Long Integer			Unique primary key
Title	Text	4	Mr	
Surname	Text	25		Mandatory
Initials	Text	3		Must be uppercase
Street	Text	30		
Village	Text	30		
Town	Text	30		
County	Text	20	Suffolk	
PostCode	Text	10		Must be uppercase
HomeTelephone	Text	15		
WorkTelephone	Text	20		
SalesCustomer	Yes/No		No	
FramingCustomer	Yes/No		No	
RestorationCustomer	Yes/No		No	
TapestryCustomer	Yes/No		No	
ExhibitionCustomer	Yes/No		No	
BusinessCustomer	Yes/No		No	Must be Yes if BusinessName not empty
BusinessName	Text	30		
CustomerNotes	Memo			

Figure 3.2: The tblCustomer table

JOB   (Table name: **tblJob**)

Attribute Name	Data Type	Max. Length	Default value	Description/ Validation
JobNo*	Long Integer			Unique primary key
CustomerID	Long Integer			Must exist on Customer table
Orderdate	Date			
JobValue	Currency			Calculated field (Total of individual item values)
ItemsInJob	Integer		1	The number of items on this Job sheet
JobNotes	Memo			

Figure 3.3: The tblJob table

ITEM   (Table name: **tblItem**)

Attribute Name	Data Type	Max. Length	Default value	Description/ Validation
ItemNo*	Integer		1	Must be numeric (ItemNo and JobNo constitute the unique primary key)
JobNo*	Long Integer			Must exist on tblJob table
ItemType	Text	11		Must be one or more of Sales, Framing, Exhibition, Tapestry or Restoration
ArtistName	Text	20		Only entered if Sale or Exhibition customer
SubjectMatter	Text	20		Description of painting sold, e.g. Dogs, Landscape
ItemValue	Currency			Price charged for Sale/Job
ItemDescription	Text	30		
Frame	Text	20		Type and/or colour of frame

Figure 3.4: The tblItem table

Naming conventions

There are various conventions for naming the objects that you use. You don't have to use a naming convention but it will certainly make your database easier to create and maintain, and will probably earn you extra marks in project work. Shown below are the Leszynski/Reddick naming conventions, which will be used in this book.

Level 1

Object	Tag	Example
Table	tbl	tblCustomer
Query	qry	qryClientName
Form	frm	frmCustomer
Report	rpt	rptSales
Macro	mcr	mcrUpdateList
Module	bas	basIsNotLoaded

Level 2

Object	Tag	Example
Table	tbl	tblCustomer
Table (lookup)	tlkp	tlkpRegion
Table (system)	zstbl	zstblUser
Query (select)	qry	qryClientName
Query (append)	qapp	qappNewPhone
Query (crosstab)	qxtb	qxtbYearSales
Query (delete)	qdel	qdelOldCases
Query (form filter)	qflt	qfltAlphaList
Query (lookup)	qlkp	qlkpSalary
Query (make table)	qmak	qmakSaleTo
Query (system)	zsqry	zsqryMacroName
Query (update)	qupd	qupdDiscount
Form	frm	frmCustomer
Form (dialogue)	fdlg	fdlgInputDate
Form (menu)	fmnu	fmnuMain
Form (message)	fmsg	fmsgCheckDate
Form (subform)	fsub	fsubInvoice
Report	rpt	rptTotals
Report (subreport)	rsub	rsubValues
Report (system)	zsrpt	zsrptMacroName
Macro	mcr	mcrUpdateList
Macro (for form)	m[formname]	m[formname]Customer
Macro (menu)	mmnu	mmnuStartForm
Macro (for report)	m[rptname]	m[rptname]Totals
Macro (system)	zsmcr	zsmcrLoadLookUp
Module	bas	basTimeScreen
Module (system)	zsbas	zsbasAPIcall

Figure 3.5: Leszynski/Reddick naming conventions

Data validation

Any item of data that will be input by the user will be prone to error. As far as possible, you want to make sure that the program will not 'crash' (terminate unexpectedly) whatever the user enters.

In addition, various checks can be made to specific fields such as range checks, checks for particular characters (e.g. Y or N), checks that a particular record exists and so on. You have to try and anticipate all the errors that users might make and prevent them from making them, or give them a chance to correct the error before the computer accepts the data.

Data validation is an important aspect of your project, and will earn you extra marks if it is carefully planned and explained. In your report, discuss the reasons for the validations you have chosen.

Checklist of facts to record about each data item

- Name (Note that while Access refers to 'field names', in database terminology fields are referred to as 'attributes'.);
- Data type e.g. alphanumeric, integer, real, or logical (Boolean);
- Length (if text);
- Default value;
- Plain language description;
- Validation checks.

Output

Referring back to the analysis, the following output is to be produced:

1. **List of Business customers.**
   The fields to be included are Customer name and address, Name of Business.
2. **List of customers interested in a particular artist or subject.**
   The fields to be included are Customer name and address.
3. **List of customers whose total jobs exceed a given value.**
   The user will enter a value, e.g. £100 and the report will produce a list of all customers whose total jobs exceed this amount. The fields to be included are Customer name and address, and total job value.
4. **A Mail merge facility to send letters to selected customers.**
5. **Mailing labels.**

Rather than designing each report manually using pencil and paper, it may be quicker to prototype a solution and include screenshots of each report layout. Then annotate this to show what changes you need to make to get the report into its final form.

The user interface

Data entry screens

If you are using MS Access, 'wizards' may be used for the initial screen creation, and the screens customised so that they look attractive and are easy to use. As most people design screens in this way rather than with paper and pencil, it is acceptable to include a sample prototype screenshot in the Design Section, annotated to show your design rationale, and with proposed alterations and extra features sketched in by hand. Do **not** simply include screenshots of your screens in their final implemented form. Take the screenshots early on while you are in the prototyping stage and annotate by hand with your design ideas before proceeding to implement them. It may be wise to save your prototype screens under different names so that you can print a new screenshot whenever you need one.

Tip: In Windows, pressing **Alt** and **Print Screen** together will place a copy of the active window in the Clipboard, from where it may be pasted into a Word document or into a Paint program for editing. Pressing **Print Screen** alone captures the entire screen. Alternatively, you can use one of the many screen capture utility programs available.

Guidelines for screen design

There are many good books written on the subject of screen design, but a few commonsense rules will go a long way.

- be sensible in your use of colour. Dark blue text on a black background is almost illegible, yellow on green is merely unpleasant.

- use both uppercase and lowercase. All-uppercase sentences are harder to read, and less attractive.

- be consistent in your terminology: for example on menu screens, use Q for 'Quit' on every menu, not E for 'Exit' on some, and '5. Return to main menu' on others.

- don't use obscure error messages such as 'Error X551'. Where possible, replace built-in system error messages with your own more explicit messages.

- help the user wherever possible. For example, the instruction 'Enter date' with no clue as to the correct format may leave the user floundering. Give an on-screen example of the required format, such as dd/mm/yy.

Menu structures

Most projects will probably start by displaying a menu of options from which the user may choose, and some of these choices may lead to submenus. Use the following guidelines when designing your menus:

- Each menu should be given a title which uniquely identifies it, such as 'Main Menu', 'Reports Menu' and so on.

- The heading on each submenu should display the choice that was made on the previous menu, so that the user always has a clear idea of what option is currently operative. For example, if the user selects 'Reports Menu' from the main menu, the next menu should be headed 'Reports Menu'.

- The last option on each menu should take the user back to the previous level of menu.

When you have decided on your menu structure, you should draw up an outline chart showing movement between menus, and include this in your project report. An example is given below.

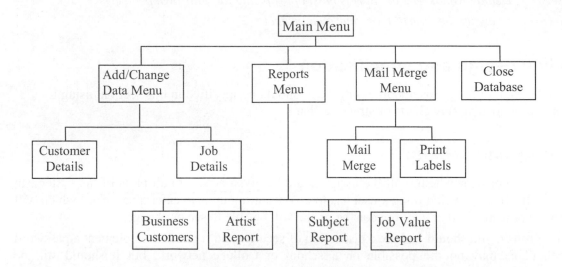

Figure 3.6: Chart showing movement between menus

Charts showing overall systems design

This refers to systems flowcharts, system outline charts or other types of system chart, **not** program flowcharts.

The NCC (National Computing Centre) suggests using the following symbols in systems flowcharts:

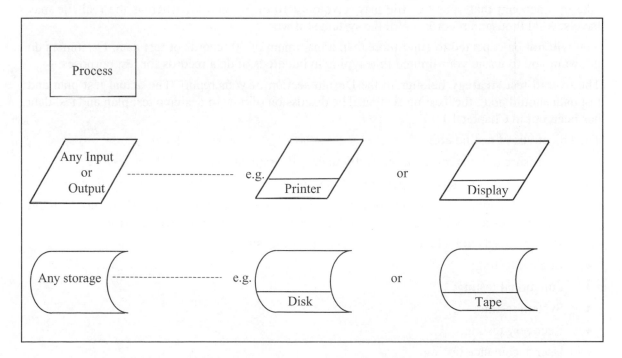

Figure 3.7: Systems flowchart symbols

A systems flowchart and system outline chart for the specimen project is shown in Part 3.

Pause: *Decide which type of chart is most appropriate for your own project.*
Action: *Draw up the chart(s) for your own project.*

Module design and specification

Detailed design of programs, modules or macros should be specified in this section, using for example pseudocode, flowcharts or structure charts.

Security and backup

You need to consider whether all the users should be given access to all parts of the system. In many applications, the first thing a user has to do on starting up is to enter a password which will determine how much, if any, of the data he or she will be able to see or change.

In your project, you should include a discussion of security and if possible implement a password system. (This may not be possible on a school or College network, but it should still be considered in your report.)

Methods and frequency of backup should also be considered; you could include an option on one of the user menus, or describe how to do a backup of the data in your user manual.

Designing a test strategy

It may seem strange to start thinking about testing before you have even started coding, but in fact it is an essential task if everything is going to work correctly once it is installed. You must also take into account that your test file may have only 10 or 20 records, whereas the real file may have several thousand records. Will the system still work?

You will not be expected to enter more than a maximum of 50 records of test data. Examiners do not want you to waste your limited time typing in hundreds of data records for test purposes.

The overall test **strategy** belongs in the Design section of your report. The actual test plan and test data should go in the Testing section. The discussion of how to design a test plan and test data has been put in Chapter 10.

The objectives of testing are:

♦ To ensure the system works correctly under all circumstances

♦ To ensure that all systems perform all the functions listed in the original specification.

At all stages of testing, there should be a positive attempt to **provoke** system failure, not to avoid it. (Remember, a successful test is one which uncovers a hitherto undiscovered error.)

A test strategy needs to include different types of testing, such as:

♦ Logical testing;

♦ Functional testing;

♦ System testing;

♦ Recovery testing;

♦ User acceptance testing.

These are explained in more detail below.

Logical testing

This involves designing test data to test every path in the system at least once. For a project implemented in Access, this could include the following:

♦ As each input form is completed, every field is tested with both valid and invalid data. Particular attention is paid to validation procedures, default values, tab order and any special features.

♦ Accepted data is stored in the database for use in queries and reports.

♦ Each macro and code module is tested as soon as it is written, using sufficient data to ensure that all statements have been tested at least once.

♦ Sufficient data is added to test all aspects of queries and reports, including any 'exception' cases such as 'No matching records found' in a query.

♦ Sufficient data is added to ensure that some reports are more than 1 page in length, to ensure that the page layout on the second page is satisfactory.

♦ Reports are created specifically to provide hard copy of test data used so that the expected results of queries and calculations can be compared with the actual results.

♦ All menus, password routines and exits from the program are tested.

♦ When bugs are discovered and/or changes are made, the object (e.g. form, query, report) is tested again with valid and invalid data, bearing in mind that a change in one place sometimes has an unexpected effect in another area of the program.

Functional testing

The purpose of functional testing is to ensure that the program performs all the functions that were originally specified, that all the input is correctly accepted, output correctly produced, and files or tables correctly updated. It relates to the whole system and does not require a technical understanding of the system.

♦ All the functions of the system as originally specified are systematically tested to ensure that nothing has been accidentally omitted or misinterpreted.

♦ A positive attempt is made to anticipate errors that an inexperienced user might make, and tests are made to check the effect of such errors and ensure that they do not result in incorrect actions or bad data being stored in the database.

System testing

♦ On completion of the whole system, each aspect of it is retested to ensure no errors have been introduced.

♦ The system is tested with a realistic amount of data; although you are not expected to spend days typing in hundreds of records, you should test the system with about 50 records in each of the main tables.

Recovery testing

♦ 'Recovery testing' can be carried out to determine what happens if, for example, there is a power cut in the middle of data entry. (Is the whole database corrupted? If so you'd better warn the user to make frequent backups!)

Acceptance testing

♦ The user is invited to test the system to ensure that it fulfills the stated objectives. (If possible, observe this testing but do not stop the user from making mistakes – your system should cope with unexpected user behaviour!)

Summary

This chapter has emphasised the importance of careful **design** of a system, involving:

♦ looking closely at the desired **output** in order to determine the **input** and **processes** required to produce it;

♦ giving careful attention to the user interface, including design of input/output forms and reports;

♦ identifying and incorporating any required data validation;

♦ choosing and justifying appropriate file structures and data structures;

♦ planning, in outline, the overall system design. This will show how each part of the system will work using diagrammatic techniques such as system outline charts, charts showing movement between menus, systems flow charts, structure or hierarchy charts or other appropriate methods;

♦ considering measures to protect the security and integrity of the data;

♦ designing a test strategy.

You should look closely at the specification for your Examination Board. This will list in detail what is to go into each section of the report.

Chapter 4 – Prototyping

Objectives

By the end of this chapter you will have:

created tables;

defined relationships;

created input forms;

created reports;

performed a mail merge to selected customers;

created mailing labels;

implemented a menu structure;

built a prototype solution for the specimen project.

Why prototype?

Using MS Access, it does not take very long to create all the tables, input forms, menus and reports needed for the final system. You may decide not to spend any more time on the implementation, other than changing a few colours, headings, and field labels, and hand in the project without doing any further customisation. However, be warned that without doing some programming of modules or macros, it will be almost impossible to get an A grade at A Level, though the project may be quite adequate at AS Level.

Once you have built a prototype, it may be obvious what improvements could be made, and most of these will probably involve some programming, even if it is just to calculate a few totals, maximise an input form, or automatically increment a CustomerID. It will be well worth learning how to write modules in Visual Basic to turn your project into a really usable system.

Building a prototype for the specimen project

In this chapter you will be taken through the steps to create the required tables, relationships, input forms, reports and menus. It is assumed that you have some familiarity with the basics in MS Access. The prototype was built using Access 2000 for Windows 98, but the steps are similar using Access 7 for Windows 95 and Access 2 for Windows 3.1.

> **When the three versions differ in more than minor detail, separate instructions for Access 7 & Access 2 are shown in *italics*.**

Creating a new database

- Start Access.
- Create a new database using Blank Database.
  Access 2: Select File, New Database.
- In the File New Database dialogue box, select the pathname, for example
  - 3½ Floppy (A:)
  in the Save In box. Enter the filename (e.g. *ABFrames*) in the File Name box.
  Access 2: In Drives, enter the drive name, e.g. A: and in Directories, select a directory.

Creating the database tables

Step 1: Creating the tblCustomer table

- In the main database window, click the **Tables** tab and then click **New**.
- In the dialogue box which appears, select **Design View**, and click **OK**.
  Access 2: Select New Table.
- Define fields as shown below in Figure 4.1. Note that the CustomerID has been given a type Number, and in the Field Size parameter in the lower half of the screen, it is defined as Long Integer. Refer back to Figure 3.2 to give the text fields the correct length.
- Put the cursor in the **Title** field, and then move it to the **Default Value** property in the bottom half of the screen. Enter *"Mr"* (include the quotation marks.)
- Similarly, set the default value of the **County** field to *"Suffolk"*.
- Define **CustomerID** as the key field by highlighting the row and selecting the Key icon on the toolbar.
- Save the table as *tblCustomer*.

The Key icon

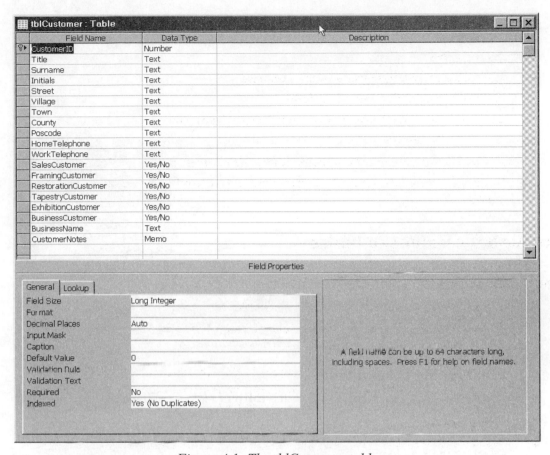

Figure 4.1: The tblCustomer table

Step 2: Creating the tblJob table

- Follow the same procedure to create the **tblJob** table (see Figure 4.2). Be sure to use the correct data types for each field, e.g. **Short Date** for the Orderdate field, **Memo** for the JobNotes field, **Integer** for ItemsInJob.

- Define **JobNo** as the key field, and save the table as *tblJob*.

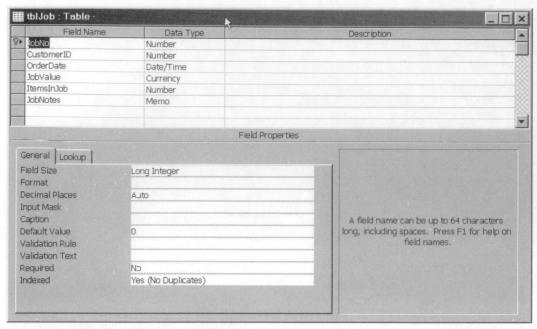

Figure 4.2: The tblJob table

Step 3: Creating the tblItem table

- Follow the same procedure to create the **tblItem** table (see Figure 3.4 and 4.3). Use **Currency** as the data type for the ItemValue field.

- Define **ItemNo** and **JobNo** as the joint key field, by highlighting both rows and selecting the Key icon.

- Save the table as *tblItem*.

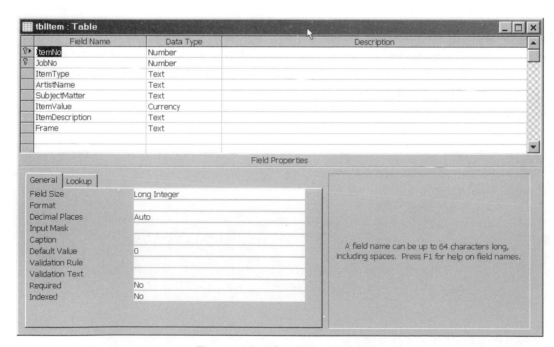

Figure 4.3: The tblItem table

Defining relationships between tables

Relationships tool

- With all the tables closed, click on the Relationships tool in the Toolbar.

- Add the tables **tblCustomer**, **tblJob** and **tblItem** in that order, and click **Close**. The tables appear in the Relationships window; if you have added them in a different order, drag them until they appear as in Figure 4.4.

- Create a one-to-many relationship between **tblCustomer** and **tblJob** by dragging CustomerID from tblCustomer onto CustomerID in tblJob.

   (N.B. Always drag from the **one** to the **many** side of the relationship – i.e. **one** customer has **many** jobs.)

- Check **Enforce Referential Integrity** to ensure that it is impossible to enter a job for a non-existent customer, and check **Cascade Delete Related Records** to ensure that if you delete a customer, all jobs for that customer will automatically be deleted. Click the **Create** button.

- Create a one-to-many relationship between **tblJob** and **tblItem** by dragging JobNo from tblJob on to JobNo in tblItem.

- Check **Enforce Referential Integrity** to ensure that it is impossible to enter an item for a non-existent job, and check **Cascade Delete Related Records** to ensure that if you delete a job, all items for that job will automatically be deleted. Click the **Create** button.

- Close the relationships window, making sure the relationships are saved.

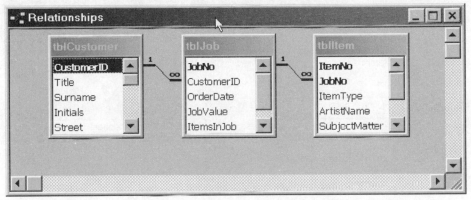

Figure 4.4: Creating the relationships between the three tables

Creating a form for entering Customer details

- From the main database window, select the **Forms** tab and click **New**. Select **Autoform: Columnar** to create the Input form, specifying **tblCustomer** as the table where the object's data comes from (Figure 4.5). Click on OK.

   Access 2: From the main database window, select Form, New. In the next dialogue box, click the down arrow beside the 'Select a Table/Query' box and select tblCustomer. Then click Form Wizards. In the next dialogue box, select Autoform.

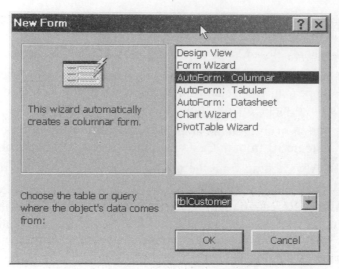

Figure 4.5: Creating the frmCustomer Input form

- Save the form as *frmCustomer*. It will appear something like the one shown in Figure 4.6.

  Access 2: The fields are set out differently, with a form heading created automatically by the wizard.

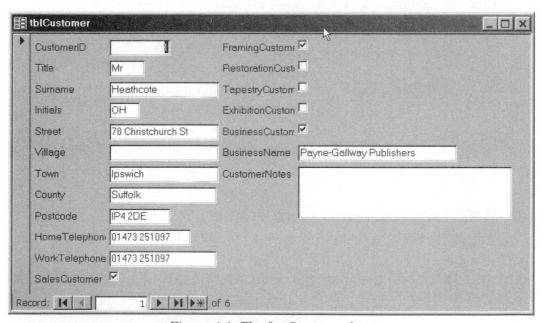

Figure 4.6: The frmCustomer form

- Switch to Design View by clicking the Design View icon.
- Create space in the form's header area by dragging the Header line downwards.

  Access 2: Omit this step.

- Place a text box by clicking the Label icon, and then clicking and dragging where the heading Customer Details Form is to appear. (Hint: if the toolbox

Design View icon

Label icon
(Access 2000, Access 7)

toolbar disappears, try clicking the **frmCustomer** tab at the bottom of the screen (Windows 98).

Access 2: Omit this step.

• Type the text *Customer Details Form*. You can alter its size, justification and font if you like.

• Rearrange the fields on the form by dragging them, so that the form looks something like the one shown in Figure 4.7.

• Save and close the form.

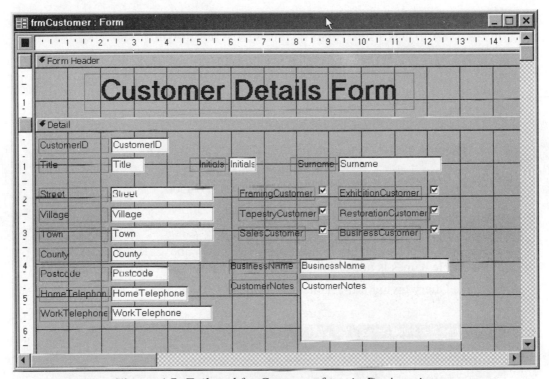

Figure 4.7: Tailored frmCustomer form in Design view

Creating a form for entering Job details

Before you start this form, look back at Figure 2.1 to see what the job sheet looks like in the current manual system. The owners have specified that they do not want all these details on the new computerised job sheet, as they will still be writing out job orders manually, and transferring the information to the computer about once a week. The data required on each job is

    Job number and order date
    Customer name and address
    Number of items in job
    Total job value

and for each item in a particular job:

    Type of item (sales, restoration, framing etc.)
    Item value
    Type of frame (if framing item)
    Artist name and subject matter (if sales)

Step 1: Creating a query to combine data from two tables

The data comes from 3 different tables: **tblCustomer**, **tblJob**, and **tblItem**. The first step is to create and save a query that will combine fields from tblCustomer and tblJob. The main form will use the resulting table (dynaset) as the source for the main form. That way, as soon as you enter the CustomerID for an existing customer, the name and address will be automatically displayed. The items for each job will be entered and listed on a subform.

- From the database window, click the **Queries** tab and select **New**.
- In the New Query dialogue box, select **Design View**. Click **OK**.

  Access 2: Click New Query

- In the Show Table *(Add Table)* dialogue box, add **tblCustomer** and **tblJob**, then close the dialogue box.

- Place the following three sets of fields in the table shown at the bottom of the screen (see Figure 4.8) by double-clicking them or dragging them in the following order:

tblJob:	JobNo, OrderDate, CustomerID
tblCustomer:	Title, Initials, Surname, Street, Village, Town, County, Postcode
tblJob:	JobValue, ItemsInJob, JobNotes

  (Be sure to place each field from the table shown above. If the row showing the Table names is not visible, select **View**, **Table Names** from the menu.)

- Save the Query giving it the name *qryCustomerJob*, and then close it.

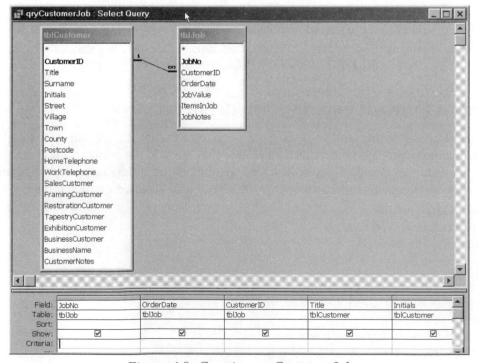

Figure 4.8: Creating qryCustomerJob

Step 2: Creating a form with a subform * (See different steps below for Access 2)

- As each job may consist of several items, the data entry form for jobs will contain a subform listing each item. Start by selecting **Forms**, **New** from the database window, and in the New Form dialogue box, select **Form Wizard** in the list.

- In the **Tables/Queries** list box select **qryCustomerJob**.

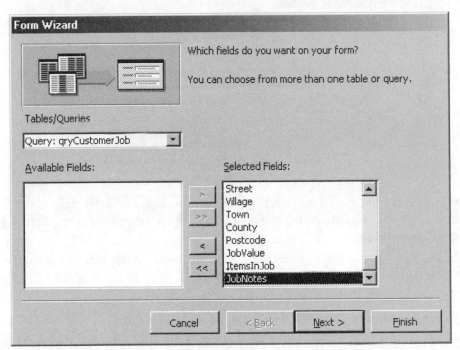

Figure 4.9: Creating the frmJobSheet with subform for Items

- In the first wizard dialogue box, click the double arrow >> to select all the fields from the list of available fields in the qryCustomerJob query. Then, select the **tblItem** table in the Table/Queries box. All the fields from tblItem should appear on the form, except JobNo, because this will already be on the main form. Click the double arrow >> to add all the fields from this table to the Selected Fields box, then highlight **JobNo** (make sure it's the one from tblItem, not qryCustomerJob, and click the back arrow < to put it back in the left hand box. (Figure 4.10)

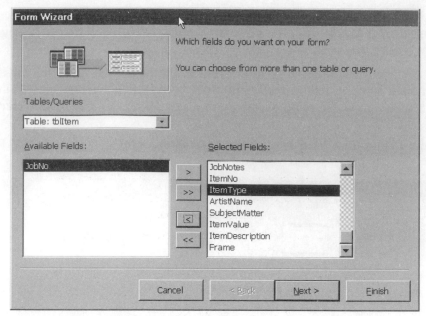

Figure 4.10: Selecting fields for inclusion on the Job sheet

- Click **Next**, and if you have set up the relationships correctly before starting this step, the wizard asks you how you want to view your data. Select **by qryCustomerJob**.

- In the same wizard dialogue box, select the **Form with subform(s)** option. Click **Next**.

- Select **Datasheet View** for the subform. Click **Next**.

- Select **Standard** style in the next dialogue box. Click **Next**.

- Give your form the title *frmJobSheet*, and the subform the title *fsubItems*. When you click **Finish**, Microsoft Access creates two forms, one for the main form and one for the subform.

- Open the form for data entry. It should look much like the one shown in Figure 4.11.

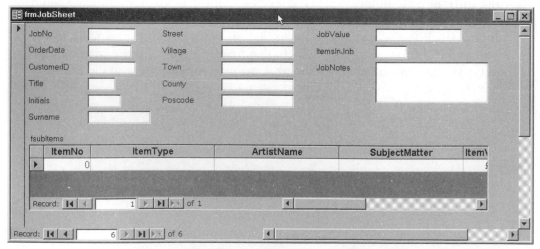

Figure 4.11: The frmJobSheet data entry form

Step 2 (Access 2: Creating a form with a subform)

- *As each job may consist of several items, the data entry form for jobs will contain a subform listing each item. Start by selecting Form, New from the database window.*

- *In the New Form dialogue box, select qryCustomerJob query in the Select a Table/Query list box. Then click Form Wizards.*

- *In the Form Wizards dialogue box, select Main/Subform and click OK.*

- *In the Main/Subform Wizard dialogue box, select tblItem as the table or query which contains data for the subform. Click Next.*

- *Click the double arrow to select all the fields from the list of available fields in the qryCustomerJob query. Click Next.*

- *Click the double arrow >> to select all the fields from the tblItem table for inclusion in the subform. We want all these fields except JobNo, as this will already appear on the main form, so highlight JobNo and click the back arrow < to remove it from the selection. Click Next.*

- *In answer to the question 'Which table contains a field that is in both the main form and the subform?', select tblJob. Click next.*

- *Select Standard style. Click Next.*

- *Give your form the title 'frmJobSheet'. Leave the default option 'Open the form with data in it' selected. Click Finish.*

- *A message appears 'You must save the subform before the Main/Subform Wizard can proceed.' Click OK.*

- *Give your subform the name 'fsubItems'. Click OK.*

- *A message appears 'The Main/Subform wizard couldn't establish a link between the main form and the subform,' Click OK. (The link has to be created by specifying the common field in each form, which you'll do below.)*

- *The form opens ready for data entry.*

- *In Design view, arrange the fields in a more suitable format (see Figure 4.12).*

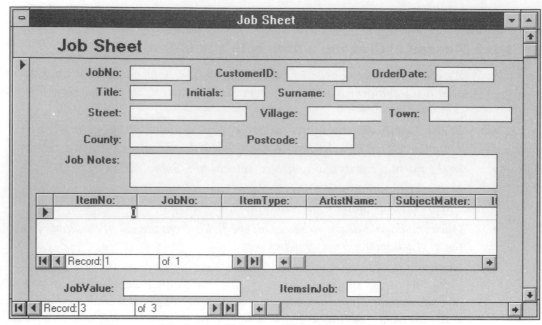

Figure 4.12: frmJobSheet created in Access 2

- *You now have to link the fsubItems subform to the Main form. Click the fsubItems subform with the right mouse button to display a popup menu. Click Properties.*

- *In the 'Link Child Fields' property, type JobNo.*

- *In the 'Link Master Fields' property, type JobNo. (This is the name of the common field in both the tblItem table and the qryCustomerJob query).*

- *Save the form as 'frmJobSheet'.*

Testing the data entry forms

You can start work on your test plan at this stage, although it will be worked out in more detail later on. You should try entering invalid as well as valid data. What happens when you try to enter a customer with an ID that already exists on file, or a non-numeric customer ID?

1. Enter about 6 customers, with CustomerIDs 1 to 6, using the **frmCustomer** data entry form.

    Be sure to include some in each category (sales, framing, etc.) A customer may belong to more than one category.

2. Open the **frmJobSheet** data entry form and enter one or two jobs for at least three customers, using job numbers starting at 101, for example. Some jobs should contain two or three items – for example a restoration and a framing.

Again, note what happens when you try to enter a job for a non-existent customer, a duplicate job number, or an invalid date.

Start making notes about the weaknesses of these forms. For example:

♦ the job total and number of items in job should be calculated and entered automatically.

♦ how will you find all the jobs for one customer (one of the user's stated requirements)?

♦ when a job is to be entered, how will you be able to find out whether the customer is already on file and if so, what his/her ID is?

Creating and saving queries to select different categories of customer

Step 1: Creating the query to select all business customers

- From the database window, select **Query, New**. Choose **Design View** to create the query from scratch.

  Access 2: Select New Query, not Query Wizard.

- In the Show Table dialogue box, select **tblCustomer** and click **Add**. Close the Show Table dialogue box.

- Double-click each of the fields from **CustomerID** down to **WorkTelephone**, plus the **BusinessCustomer** field, to select them.

- Set the criteria for **BusinessCustomer** to **Yes**. You can deselect **Show**, since this field will simply be Yes for all the selected customers.

- You can set the **Sort** criteria to **Ascending** on Customer Surname and Initials to show the customers in alphabetical order of surname and initials.

- Run the query to make sure it works properly, and then save it as *qryBusinessCustomer*.

Run tool

Step 2: Creating the queries to select customers interested in a particular artist, etc.

For the prototype, it is sufficient to show how one query is created. The other queries will be added in the final version.

Creating a report listing all business customers

- From the database window, select **Report, New**.

- In the New Report dialogue box, select **qryBusinessCustomer** as the query where the object's data comes from, and double-click **AutoReport: Tabular**.

  Access 2: Select qryBusinessCustomer in the 'Select a Table/Query' list box and click Report Wizards. Click Next.

  Select Tabular. Click Next.

  Click the double arrow >> to select all the fields for the report. Click Next.

  There is no need to set a Sort Order, so click Next again.

  Select Portrait view, and click Next

  Give the report a title 'rptBusinessCustomer' and select 'See all the fields on one page'. Click Finish.

- The wizard automatically creates the report, which will appear with data shown, as in figure 4.13.

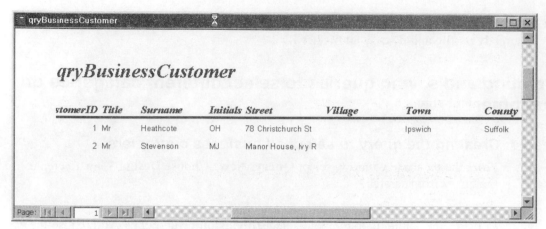

Figure 4.13: The rptBusinessCustomer report

- The report needs tidying up. Switch to Design view and see if you can get it to look more like the report shown in Figure 4.14.

- Save it as *rptBusinessCustomer*.

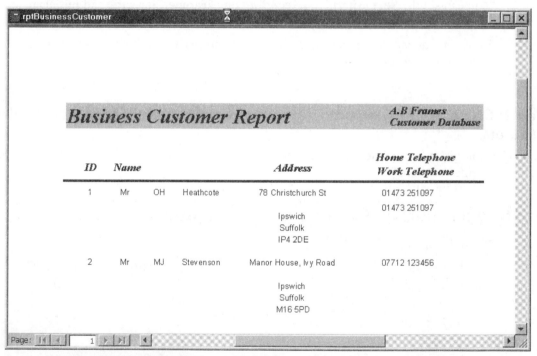

Figure 4.14: The final version of the rptBusinessCustomers report

Creating mailing labels for all business customers

- From the database window, select **Report**, **New**.

- In the New Report dialogue box, select **qryBusinessCustomer** as the query where the object's data comes from, and double-click **Label Wizard**.

    Access 2: In the Report Wizard Dialogue box, select Mailing Label. The procedure is somewhat different from that described in the next few steps (you construct the label at the start), but the instructions are easy to follow.

- In the Label Wizard dialogue box, specify the dimensions of your label. Accept the default settings, or change them if you wish to experiment.

- In the next dialogue box, select a font and font size (10 or 12 is suitable).

- In the next dialogue box, construct your label as shown in Figure 4.15.

- Continue through the remaining dialogue boxes, saving your label report as *rptBusinessCustomerLabels*. You will then be able to preview your labels on screen.

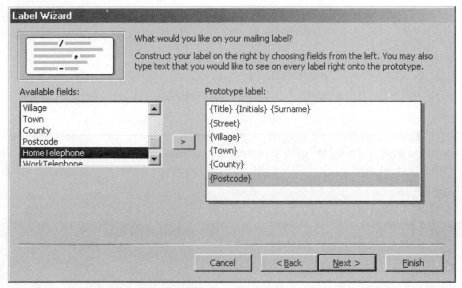

Figure 4.15: Creating mailing labels

Creating a mail merge letter

The standard letter that will be mailed to all selected customers has to be created in Word. This can be done in either of two ways; by opening Word, and then specifying the data source in your Access database (e.g. qryBusinessCustomer), or by first specifying the source and then using the OfficeLinks option in Access to open Word automatically. We'll do that now.

- From the database window, click the **Queries** tab and click **qryBusinessCustomer** to select it. This will be the source of names and addresses for the mail merge.

- Press the arrow to the right of the OfficeLinks tool. From the popup menu, select **Merge It**.

  Access 2: Click the Office Links tool.

OfficeLinks tool

- The Microsoft Word Mail Merge Wizard dialogue box opens. Select the second option: **Create a new document and then link the data to it**.

- Word opens ready to create the standard letter. Press Enter about 6 times to leave some space at the top of the letter for a standard letterhead, inserting the date, etc.

- Click the **Insert Merge Field** button in the menu bar. The field list is displayed.

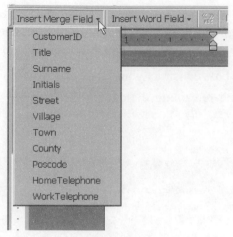

Figure 4.16: Inserting merge fields

- Click **Title**. The field <<Title>> is placed in your letter. Place the other fields for name and address, leaving spaces and pressing Enter for each new line. The actual text of the letter will be altered by the user. Your letter should appear something like Figure 4.17.

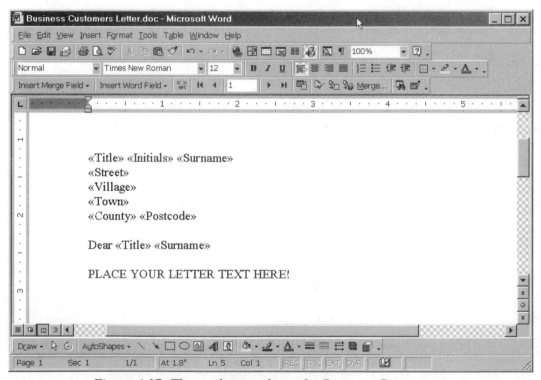

Figure 4.17: The mail merge letter for Business Customers

- Select **Tools**, **Mail Merge** and click **Step 3: Merge**.
- In the next dialogue box, click **Merge**. A letter appears for each selected customer, which can be printed (no need to do that now).

- Close without saving – you do not need to keep the letters, which are distinct from the master letter where the merge fields were placed. Save this document as *Business Customers Letter* or some other suitable title, in a convenient directory. (It may be a good idea to save the letter in the same folder as the database).

Providing the user with instructions for performing a mail merge

Instead of completely automating the mail merge, one option is simply to have clear instructions on how to print the letters, either in the User Manual, or displayed on the screen when the Mail Merge option is chosen from the menu, or both.

You should first try out the steps that the user will have to perform to use an existing standard letter, and then write instructions on how to do it. You can then create a new form to display these instructions, which will be opened when the user selects Mail Merge from your menu.

This is not included in this prototype version of the system, but you could do it as an exercise.

Creating the menu system

Look back at Figure 3.6. This shows the menu structure that we need to create.

Step 1: Creating the Add/Change Data menu

- In the database window, click the **Forms** tab and select **New**.
- In the New Form dialogue box, double-click **Design View** to create a new form without using the Wizard. Leave the Table or Query box blank.

  Access 2: Select Blank Form.
- A new blank form will appear. Click the Label tool and click and drag the cursor on the form where you want a heading to appear. Type the heading *Add/Change Data Menu*, and adjust the font style, size and position if necessary.

Label tool

- Make sure the Control Wizards tool is selected on the toolbar. Click the Command Button icon, and click and drag the cursor on the form as before.
- The first Command Button wizard dialogue box will automatically appear. Select **Form Operations, Open Form**. Click **Next**.
- Specify **frmCustomer** as the form to be opened. Click **Next**.
- Check the option button **Open the form and show all records**.

  Access 2: Skip this instruction.
- Give the button the title *Customer Details*. Click **Next**.
- Name the button *OpenfrmCustomer*. Click **Finish**.
- Place another button on the form to open the Job Sheet, in the same way as already described. Your finished form should look something like Figure 4.19.
- Click on the small square at the top left hand corner, at the intersection of the ruler lines, using the RIGHT mouse button to display a popup menu. Select **Properties**.
- In the properties box, change the settings for scroll bars, record selectors, navigation buttons and border style as shown in Figure 4.18.

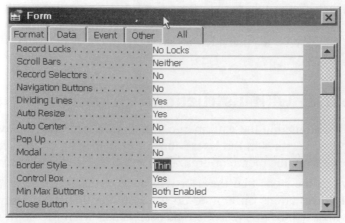

Figure 4.18: Setting the Form properties

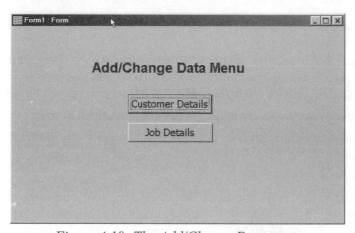

Figure 4.19: The Add/Change Data menu

- Note that a **Quit to Main Menu** option will have to be added later. Save the form as *fmnuAdd/ChangeData*.

Step 2: Creating the Reports menu

The Business Customers report is the only one to have been implemented so far, so although buttons may be placed for the other reports they will not have any actions attached to them.

- Select **Form**, **New**, and then **Design View** in the dialogue box, as before

  Access 2: Select Blank Form.

- Place a heading on the form.

- Place a command button. Select **Report Operations**, **Preview Report**. Specify **rptBusinessCustomer**.

- Continue through the other dialogue boxes, giving your button the title *Business Customers*. Change properties as before.

- Add command buttons for the Artist Report, Subject Report, Job Value Report and Return to Main Menu options. Since these buttons will not be operational yet, before you place the button you can turn off the wizard by deselecting the

Control Wizards tool

Control Wizards tool in the Design View toolbar. Then simply type the button titles straight onto the buttons.

- You can ensure that all the buttons are exactly the same size by selecting them (drag the cursor around them) and then selecting **Format**, **Size**, **to Widest**. Then repeat, selecting **to Tallest**. You can align them by selecting **Align** on the **Format** menu.

- The menu should look something like the one in Figure 4.20, but only the first button (**Business Customers**) will actually do anything. Test it now.

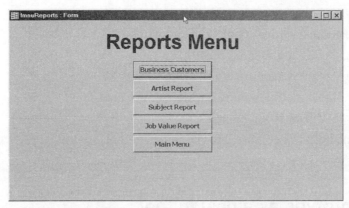

Figure 4.20: The Reports Menu

Step 3: Creating the Main Menu

Referring back to Figure 3.6, the main menu will consist of 4 items: **Add/Change Data Menu**, **Reports Menu**, **Mail Merge Menu** and **Close Database**. The first two of these have already been created. The Main menu will be created in exactly the same way, by placing Command buttons which open up the relevant submenus or close the database.

Finishing off the prototype

This step is left to you! You can complete the menu system, improve the appearance of the input screens, and add the other queries and reports. Or you can leave it just as it is, because this is sufficient to demonstrate exactly what the finished system will do.

The next step

In Part 2 of the book, this prototype has been completed without making any major changes or improvements, and a project report written up. The project has then been graded using the AQA guidelines.

In the next chapter, you will learn how to program in Visual Basic for Applications, and turn a very mediocre project into one that will earn you a top grade. You'll find the second version of the same project written up in Part 3, together with the assessment.

Summary

This chapter has covered the steps needed to build a prototype of a system which will be used in deciding upon a final design. Tables, forms, queries and reports can all be quickly built in Access using wizards.

Chapter 5 – Developing the Prototype

Objectives

By the end of this chapter you will have learned how to:

create and customise a combo box with and without using a wizard;

write a macro to find a particular record;

attach a macro to an event property of a control;

create Visual Basic modules using a variety of commands;

use variables in Visual Basic modules;

use the on-line help to get more information on command syntax.

Using the prototype as a design tool

Now that the prototype is finished, you can take a good look at it and perhaps even show it to the end-users to get their views. Look back at the original objectives and ask yourself in what ways the system as it stands now can be improved. Here are some suggestions for the A.B. Frames project:

- ◆ A combo box could be added to the **frmCustomer** form to look up any customer.

- ◆ The customer number could be automatically incremented. This could be achieved by using a **Counter** field for the CustomerID, but it can also be done using a Visual Basic module, which will make the system more flexible in that the user can, if she wishes, choose a particular ID.

- ◆ Extra touches could be added to the **frmCustomer** form to make data entry easier and quicker; for example, the cursor could skip over the **Business Name** field unless the **Business Customer** field was ticked. The customer's initials and post code could be automatically converted to uppercase. Since most customers come from Ipswich, then as soon as *Ipswich* is entered, the county could be set equal to **Suffolk**. Alternatively, the Town field could default to Ipswich and the County field could default to Suffolk.

- ◆ A button could be added to the **frmCustomer** form so that when a new customer is added, or an existing customer looked up, the **frmJobSheet** form can automatically be opened with the CustomerID, name and address displayed.

- ◆ In the **frmJobSheet** form, the Job Total and Number of Items in Job could be calculated and entered automatically.

- ◆ In the **fsubItem** subform, a list box could be used for **Item Type** so that the user simply has to select a type rather than typing it in each time. If a customer job includes an item of type **Restoration**, for example, the Customer record could then be automatically updated to tick the **Restoration** field.

♦ All the jobs for one customer could be displayed in a subform in the **frmCustomer** form. Then, when the user double-clicks a particular job number, the **frmJobSheet** form for that job could be automatically opened up.

The next step in the project is to figure out how these ideas are to be implemented, and write up the Design Section of the final report. You can turn to the Design Section of the second project to see how this has been done.

The next three chapters of this book will show you how to implement all these ideas, many of which you may be able to modify for your own project. You will learn a lot from working through them, and once you are comfortable with writing Visual Basic modules and know what the possibilities are, you will find it very much easier to come up with a good design.

However, this book is not intended to be a complete Access and Visual Basic tutorial, so if you want to become a real expert, you need to buy a good book which teaches your particular version of Access – there are dozens available.

Creating a combo box to find records

Step 1: Using a wizard to create the combo box

One of the most common tasks in any database application is looking up an existing record. Adding a combo box to do this will make this task much easier for the user than using the standard 'Find' command. To create the combo box:

- Open the **frmCustomer** form in **Design** view.

  Control Wizards tool

  In Access 2000, the Control Wizard is automatically on, but for the other versions make sure the Control Wizards tool is selected and then click the Combo Box tool.

- Click the Combo Box tool.

  Combo box tool

- Click the top of the form next to the title **Customer Details Form**. (You may need to move the heading over and enlarge the form.) The combo box wizard starts, asking how you want to get the values it will display in the list.

- Select the third option, **Find a record on my form based on the value I selected in my Combo Box**, and then click **Next**.

  Access 2: Select the first option, 'I want the combo box to look up the values in a table or query'. Click Next. In the next dialogue box, select tblCustomer, and click Next.

  A message is displayed: 'The table or query you selected to provide values for your list has more than 15 fields. The wizard will show only the first 15 fields.' Click OK.

- The wizard asks you which fields you want to include in the combo box. Double-click the **Surname** field to add it to the **Selected Fields** list, and then click **Next**.

- Drag the right side of the field selector in the **Surname** column to make it a bit narrower, and then click **Next**.

  Access 2: In the dialogue box, select the option 'Remember the value for later use'. (You don't want to store the selected surname in the surname field of the current record, which is that of a different customer.)

- The wizard asks what label you want for your combo box. Type *Find Customer* and then click **Finish**.

TIP: Typing an ampersand character before the F (&Find Customer) turns F into a 'hot' key, so that the user can activate the button either by pressing it or by pressing Alt-F.)

Step 2: Trying out the combo box

- Click the Form View button on the toolbar.

- Click the arrow next to the **Find Record** combo box. A list of names will be displayed.

  Access 2: A list of names will be displayed, but selecting one of them has no effect on the current record. Don't panic! We'll look at that problem in the next paragraph entitled 'Programming with macros'. In the meantime, continue with Step 3.

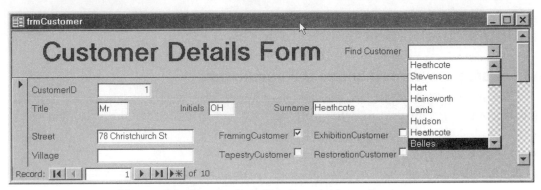

Figure 5.1: Combo box showing customer surnames

Step 3: Modifying the combo box

The combo box could be improved by displaying the names in alphabctical order, and displaying any particular surname only once even if there is more than one customer named Heathcote, say. (Later on we'll add other buttons to go to the Next or Previous record for a customer with the same surname as the one displayed.)

- Click the Design View button on the toolbar.

- With the right mouse button, click the **Find Record** combo box and then click **Properties** on the shortcut menu. The property sheet for the combo box will be displayed.

- Click the **All** tab in the property sheet to display all properties.

  Access 2: Select All Properties from the list box.

- Change the name of the combo box from **Combo41** or whatever it is now, to *FindIt*. (This will make it easier to refer to later on.)

- Click the **Row Source** property, and then click the **Build** button on the right of the property box as in Figure 5.2.

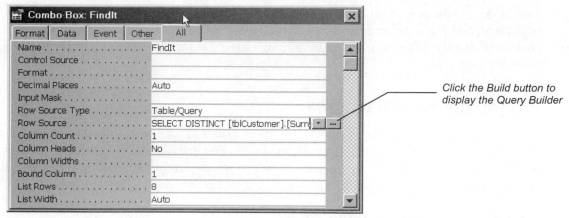

Figure 5.2: The combo box properties list

The Query Builder is displayed, and can be modified in any way you like.

Access 2: The CustomerID field does not appear in the Query.

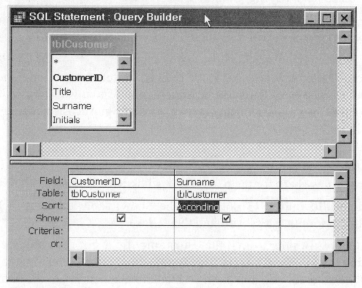

Figure 5.3: The Query Builder window for the combo box

- Click the **Sort** box underneath **Surname**, click the dropdown arrow, and then click **Ascending**.

- Close the Query Builder window, clicking **Yes** when asked if you want to save the changes to the Query and SQL statement.

- For test purposes, you should make sure you have at least two customer records for different customers with the same surname, so switch to Form View and add more customers if necessary.

- Try out the combo box. The names should be in alphabetical order, but duplicates still show up in the list.

This is far as you can go without getting into programming! The wizard has set properties and added a Visual Basic event procedure behind the scenes and what you need to do now is create your own slightly different event procedure or macro. So far, the record does not change when you click in the list.

Programming with macros

Access offers two ways to write programs; with macros and with Visual Basic. A macro consists of one or more actions, and may contain conditions that enable you to build macros containing branches and loops just like a program. Macros are generally invoked by an **event** such as opening or closing a form, clicking a button or entering or leaving a particular field.

Step 1: Placing an Unbound control

- Delete your existing Find Customer combo box, and this time, make sure the Control Wizards tool is deselected. (If your school or College network does not allow you to deselect the Control Wizards tool, don't worry.)

Control Wizards tool

- Place a combo box in the same place as before, next to the form title, and label it *Find Customer*. (If the Combo Box Wizard dialogue is displayed, press Cancel.)

- Open the properties sheet for the combo box, and name it *FindIt*.

The Row Source property now has to be defined, to tell Access where to get the values to display in the Combo Box. This can be done in one of two ways; by writing the SQL code directly into the Row Source property, or by letting Access generate the SQL from a Query. We'll do the latter.

Step 2: Defining the SQL for the Row Source

- In the properties sheet for the combo box, click **Row Source**.

- Click the **Build** button (3 dots) and the Show Table dialogue box appears. Select **tblCustomer**, press **Add** and then **Close**.

Build button

- In the Query Builder, drag the **Surname** field to the table, click **Sort**, **Ascending**, and in the **Criteria** row, type *Is Not Null*. (If a customer record has no surname entered, you don't want a blank line appearing in the combo box.)

- Close the query and answer **Yes** when prompted to save.

- Check the SQL code that has been automatically generated. With the cursor somewhere in the Row Source property, press the Zoom key (Shift-F2) and the SQL will be displayed.

  Access 2 & Access 7: when the SQL is displayed, it will say 'SELECT DISTINCTROW [tblCustomer] ... ', Access 2000 omits 'DISTINCTROW'.

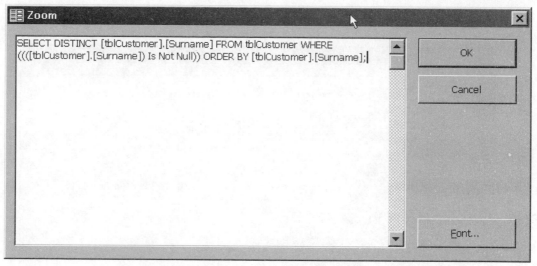

Figure 5.4: Automatically generated SQL code

- Press OK and then change to Form view to try the combo box. It will still show duplicate surnames (make sure you have some in your test data), and of course, selecting a particular surname won't have any effect because we have not yet added the appropriate event property.

- Go back to Design view and display the combo box property sheet again. Zoom in on the SQL in the Row Source, and edit it by adding in the word *DISTINCT* after SELECT (**SELECT DISTINCT [tblCustomer]**...etc), as shown above.

  Access 7 & Access 2: change DISTINCTROW to DISTINCT.

This will ensure that only one occurrence of each surname is displayed. Test your change.

Step 3: Creating a macro to find a record

- Click the Design View icon again and display the properties sheet for the combo box.

- In the **After Update** property, click the **Build** button (3 dots) and the Choose Builder window will open. Select **Macro Builder**.

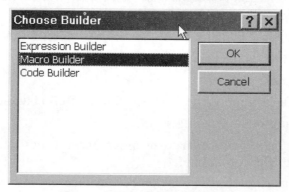

Figure 5.5: Building a macro

- In the next dialogue box, name the macro *mfrmCustomerFind*.

- The Macro Builder window will open.

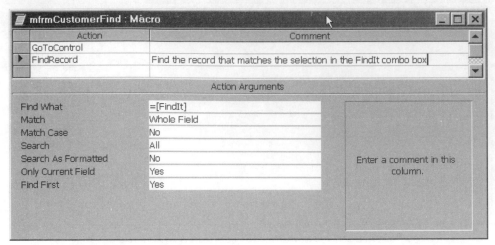

Figure 5.6: Writing a macro to find a customer record

- In the **Action** column, click the arrow and select **GoToControl**. In the Action Argument **Control Name** (in the lower half of the screen), enter *Surname*.

- On the next line in the Action column, click the arrow and select **FindRecord**. In the **Find What** Action Argument, enter *=[FindIt]*. This tells the macro to find the first record having the surname specified in the FindIt combo box.

- Add a comment to remind yourself what the macro does.

- Close the macro, answering **Yes** when asked if you want to save changes.

- Change to Form View and test the combo box.

Step 4: Add code to keep the combo box synchronised

You'll notice that when you go to a record by some means other than the combo box – by using a navigation button to go to the next record, for example, the surname displayed in the combo box doesn't change, which could confuse the user. You can add a line of code to the form's module to fix this problem.

- Open the form in Design View, or go to Design view if it is already open.

- Click the form selection box at the upper left corner of the form window (at the intersection of the rulers).

- Click the right mouse button and open the property sheet for the form.

- Click the **Event** tab in the property sheet.

  Access 2: Select Event Properties from the list box.

- Click the **On Current** property, and then click the **Build** button (3 dots).

- Select **Code Builder**, and then click OK.

- The Form module for the **frmCustomer** form opens and displays the **Form_Current** event procedure.

  Access 2: The module heading does not display the word 'Private' as shown in Figure 5.7.

- Add a line of code under the procedure heading:

```
FindIt = Surname
```

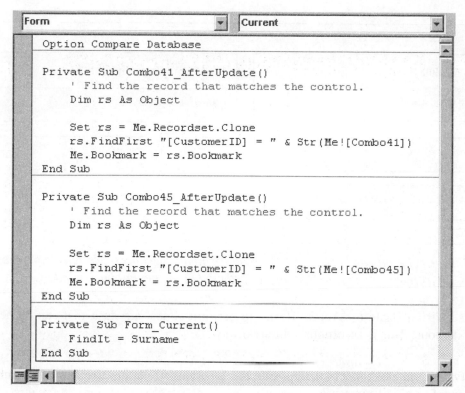

```
Form                      ▼   Current                    ▼

  Option Compare Database

  Private Sub Combo41_AfterUpdate()
      ' Find the record that matches the control.
      Dim rs As Object

      Set rs = Me.Recordset.Clone
      rs.FindFirst "[CustomerID] = " & Str(Me![Combo41])
      Me.Bookmark = rs.Bookmark
  End Sub

  Private Sub Combo45_AfterUpdate()
      ' Find the record that matches the control.
      Dim rs As Object

      Set rs = Me.Recordset.Clone
      rs.FindFirst "[CustomerID] = " & Str(Me![Combo45])
      Me.Bookmark = rs.Bookmark
  End Sub

  Private Sub Form_Current()
      FindIt = Surname
  End Sub
```

Figure 5.7: Form module

This code sets the value of the combo box (which you named **FindIt** earlier on) to the value of the **Surname** control in the current record.

- Close the module window, return to Form View and test the combo box. Perfect, or a complete disaster?

Programming in Visual Basic or Access Basic (Access 2)

The two versions of Access both use a variant of Microsoft's Visual Basic language. It is referred to as Access Basic in Access 2, and Visual Basic for Applications in subsequent versions. There are minor differences in the way that commands are written, but you will quickly get used to the format of whichever version you are using. Don't forget to use the online Help whenever you get stuck; it is invaluable!

Visual Basic (and Access Basic) code is stored in **modules**. Each form and report in a database has its own attached **form module** or **report module** for storing Visual Basic code – for example, the code attached to each control in a form is stored in the form module. (A **control** is anything in a form such as a label, data field, combo box or control button.)

Most Visual Basic code that you write will belong to an individual form or report; however, if you write code that applies to more than one form or report, you can store it in one or more **standard modules**, which are separate objects in the database window.

Visual Basic code is held in procedures, each performing a single task. A module may contain many procedures, one for each event you want to respond to, or task you want to perform. For example, a Form module may have an **Open** procedure, a **Current** procedure, an **AfterUpdate** procedure and so on. A command button on the form may have an **On Click** procedure and an **On DblClick** procedure.

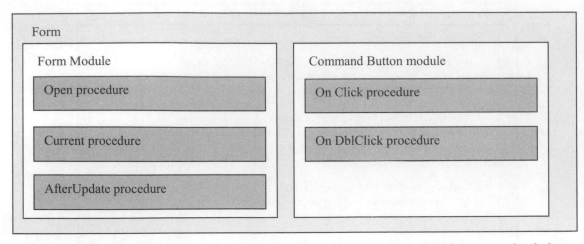

Figure 5.8: The relationship between forms, modules and procedures. Modules can also belong to reports, or be stored in a standard module in the database window.

You can use Visual Basic (or Access Basic) to perform almost any task that can be performed with macro actions. This is accomplished in two ways:

1. Equivalent statements, which duplicate the functions of certain macros. For example, the statement used in Figure 5.7

    ```
    FindIt = Surname
    ```

    is an example of an assignment statement. This could also have been written as

    ```
    Let FindIt = Surname
    ```

    The equivalent macro is the **SetValue** macro.

2. Using **methods.** Each object such as a form or control has its own set of methods. For example, to set the focus in the object Surname, you can use the **SetFocus** method, and write

    ```
    Surname.SetFocus
    ```

    DoCmd is a rather special object in Visual Basic for Applications, with its own set of methods. In Access 2, **DoCmd** is not an object, but a statement used to execute a macro action. Thus in Visual Basic, the equivalent of the **FindIt** macro action to find the first record containing "Smith" in the current field is the instruction

    ```
    DoCmd.FindRecord "Smith",,True,,True
    ```

    but in Access Basic the instruction is written

    ```
    DoCmd FindRecord "Smith",,True,,True
    ```

This action has 7 arguments (see Figure 5.6) and setting the third argument to "True" means that the search is case-sensitive; i.e. it does not find "SMITH" or "smith".

Notice that you can leave any of the arguments with their default values by omitting them, but you must remember to type a comma for each one you leave out.

Handling multiple matching records

So far, we have placed a button that finds the first record for a customer with a given surname. If this isn't the right record, the user will probably want to look at the next customer record with the same surname. We could have included more fields in the combo box, such as initials and first line of address, or we could place a **Next** button on the form. That's what we're going to do, but this time we'll use a procedure instead of a macro. Procedures are very powerful, and allow you to do things that you can't do using a macro.

Step 1: Placing a command button

- Open the **frmCustomer** form in Design View, and if necessary, make space for a command button in the **Form Header** area by dragging the **Detail** line down. (Placing the button in the Header section doesn't affect how it works, it just separates it logically from the data entry area.)

Control Wizards tool

- Make sure the Control Wizards tool is deselected, and then click the Command Button icon. Click in the header section where you want to place it. (Press Cancel if the Command Button Wizard dialogue box is displayed.)

Command Button tool

- Type the caption *Next* on the button.

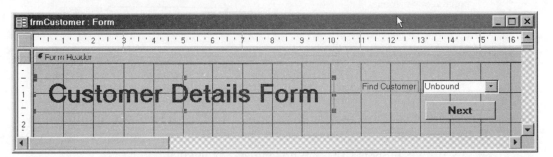

Figure 5.9: Placing the Next button

- Click the button using the right hand mouse button, and open the **Properties** box. In the **Name** property, type *Find Next*. (Note that you can have a space in a name, but when referring to it in a procedure, you must enclose it in square brackets.)

    In Access 2, be careful not to use a 'reserved word' such as FindNext, which will result in a syntax error if used in a procedure. Find Next is fine, though.

Step 2: Attaching code to locate the correct record

- Click the **On Click** event property and click the **Build** button (3 dots).
- Select **Code Builder** from the Choose Builder dialogue box.
- Type the commands as shown below. In Access 2000 other macros associated with the form will also appear in the window, but for now we're only interested in the **Find_Next_Click()** part. Note that the last argument (Find First) should be set to False because if it were left as true, the search would stop at the current record instead of finding the next record.

- Note that you can ignore case (i.e. uppercase, lowercase) when typing in Basic statements. Access checks the case and alters it if necessary when you move to the next line.

  Access 2: Type a space instead of a full stop between DoCmd and FindRecord.

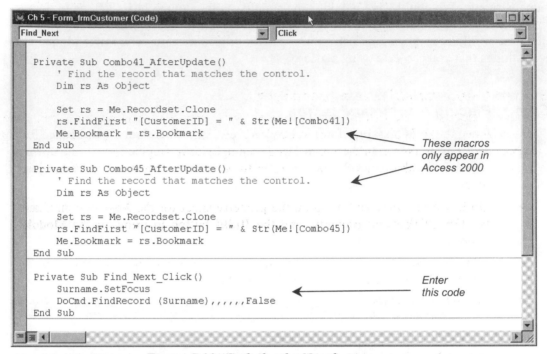

Figure 5.10: Code for the Next button

- Compile the code by clicking the Compile tool, or selecting **Compile** on the **Debug** menu at the top of the screen. This will tell you if you have any syntax errors. If there are no errors, nothing appears to happen.

- Close the module window, return to Form View and try out your button.

Compile tool

It works fine, except that when it reaches the last matching record, it might be better if it displayed a message telling the user there were no more matching records. There are various options here: a message box could be displayed, or the caption on the button could be changed to say *No more matches*, or simply *No More*. We'll try that option.

Step 3: Planning your procedure

As your procedures get longer, you will need to plan them out and write down the steps in ordinary English or pseudocode before you try and code them.

If you have tried out your **Next** button, you'll notice that when the last matching record is reached, another click has no effect; the same record remains on screen. Therefore, we can test for the last matching record by checking whether the CustomerID remains unchanged when the **Next** button is pressed. If it does, then the caption will be changed. We need to save the current CustomerID in a variable, so that it can be compared with the CustomerID in the record which becomes current when **Next** is pressed.

Here is the pseudocode for the procedure which will be executed when the **Next** button is clicked:

```
Procedure Find Next
    Save the current CustomerID in a variable called CR
    Move the cursor to the Surname field
    Find the next record with the same surname
    (If there isn't one, the same record will remain current)
    If CustomerID = CR then    (the same record is still on screen)
        change the caption on the button to "No more"
    End If
End Proc
```

Step 4: Using variables in a procedure

The above procedure requires a variable to store the current CustomerID. You should declare your variables at the beginning of the procedure, just like in a Pascal program. Like Pascal, variables declared in a procedure are *local*, known only within the procedure. The Dim statement is used to declare variables; use the online Help to get more information on variable types and rules for names.

- Go to Design view and bring up the property sheet for the **Next** button. Click the **On Click** event property, and the **Build** button to bring up the Module window.

- Edit the procedure as shown below. Note that a comment in the code is preceded by ' and has no effect on the way the code runs.

  Access 2: Remember to leave a space instead of a full stop after the DoCmd action. Otherwise the code is the same as that shown in Figure 5.11.

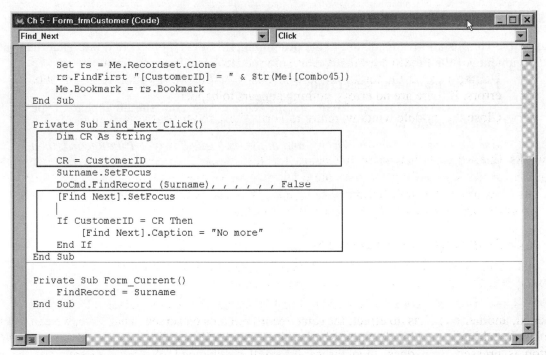

Figure 5.11: The modified code for the Next button On Click event

- Compile the code to check for syntax errors.
- Save and test the modified code.

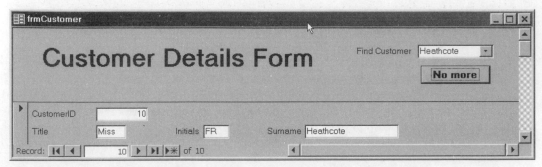

Figure 5.12: Changing the caption on the Next button

It works fine, but the only trouble is, once the caption changes to **No more**, it doesn't change back to **Next** unless you close the form and reopen it. It needs to change back as soon as the user clicks any other control. To do this, we can attach some code to the button's On Lost Focus event.

- In the property sheet for the **Next** button, click in the **On Lost Focus** property, and click the **Build** button. Select **Code Builder** in the next dialogue box and add the following line of code:

```
[Find Next].Caption = "Next"
```

- Compile and test your code. It should work perfectly!

Using the online Help in Access 2000 & Access 7

The online Help is an invaluable aid to the programmer. For example to find out what the syntax and arguments of the FindRecord method are, use the Help facility as follows:

- From the main menu select **Help**.

- Select **Microsoft Access Help**, and the 'Office Assistant' should appear. Type *Find Record* in the box where specified, then press **Search**.

   Access 7: select Answer Wizard, and in the dialogue box type FindRecord, then press Search.

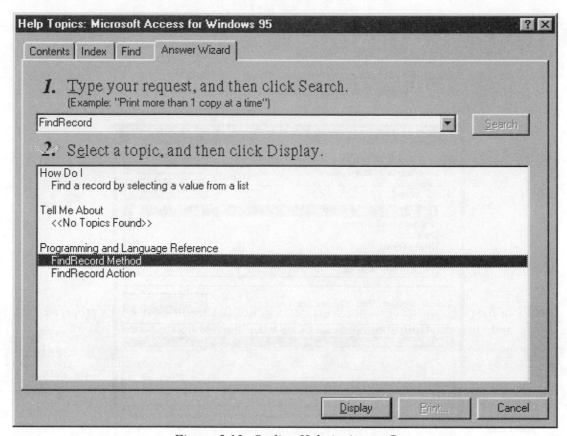

Figure 5.13: On line Help in Access 7

- **Click FindRecord Action**

  Access 7: Select FindRecord Method and press Display.

- The following screen is displayed:

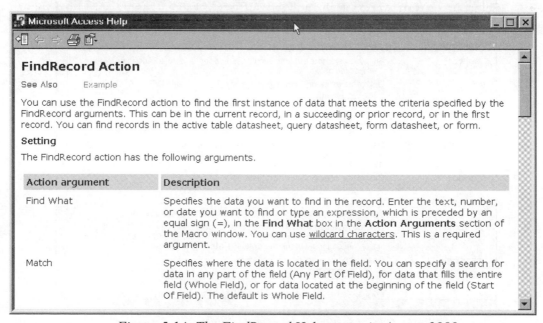

Figure 5.14: The FindRecord Help screen in Access 2000

Using the online Help in Access 2

- *From the main menu select Help.*
- *Select Search. Type the instruction you are looking for, for example FindRecord, in the dialogue box in the next screen, as shown in Figure 5.15.*

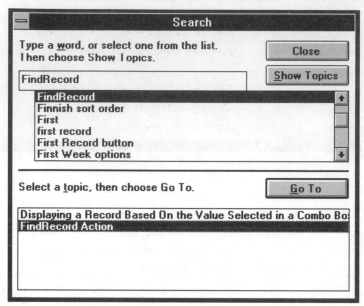

Figure 5.15: The Help screen in Access 2

- *Select FindRecord Action, and press Go To.*
- *In the FindRecord Action help screen, click Access Basic (the green hypertext at the top of the screen). The screen as shown in Figure 5.16 is displayed. Scroll down to see the rest of the screen.*

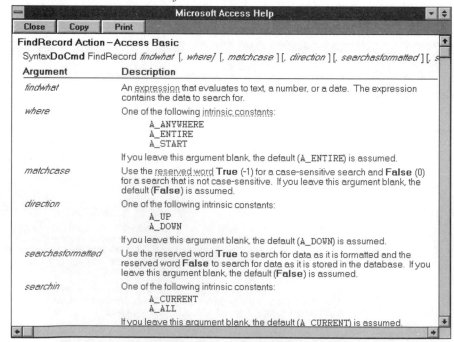

Figure 5.16: FindRecord action Help screen in Access 2

Summary

In this chapter you have begun to use macros and modules to develop a system from the prototype stage to the final product. New ways of navigating around records have been introduced, using a combo box to find a customer with a given surname, and a control button to find the next customer with the same surname.

For online information about	**On the Help menu, search for**
Creating and using combo boxes	*combo boxes*
the DoCmd method	*DoCmd* and then *carry out a macro action in a Visual Basic for Applications procedure*
Declaring variables	*Declaring variables*
If…then…else statement	*Conditional statement* or *If…Then…Else statement*
SQL statements	*SQL*

Access 2:

DoCmd	*DoCmd* and then *DoCmd statement*
Declaring variables	*Declare* and then *Dim statement* or *Type* then *Access Basic Data Types*
If…then…else	*If…then* and then *If…Then…Else statement*

You can also place the cursor on a statement and press F1 to get help on the syntax of the statement.

Chapter 6 – Optimising Data Entry

Objectives

By the end of this chapter you will have learned how to:

automatically increment the CustomerID number when adding a new record;

customise the tab order;

set the focus depending on the value(s) entered in another control;

automatically convert an entry to uppercase;

set default field values;

display values from one form in another form;

create customised error messages;

perform a calculation and display the results in a field of a form.

Providing data entry shortcuts

Data entry can be a tedious, time-consuming business, and anything you can do to make it easier will result in a more useful system for the end-user. The aim is to reduce the number of keystrokes and mouse-clicks required by anticipating the data entry wherever possible, and giving the user helpful messages immediately if they make an invalid entry. In this chapter we'll look at several different techniques which will be applicable to a great many different situations.

Automatically incrementing the CustomerID

One way of automatically incrementing a key field such as CustomerID is to make its field type **Counter**. Access then automatically assigns the next integer value whenever a new record is opened. However, this is often unsatisfactory because the number cannot bc altered, so if the user wants some control over what numbers are allocated another method has to be used.

As with all programming, you need to think out the steps involved and write them down in ordinary English or pseudocode before you start banging in code. Here is a pseudocode version:

```
Procedure AddCustomer
   Go to the last record
   Set CustID = value of CustomerID in this record
   If CustID = 0   Then              (i.e. this is the very first record)
     CustomerID = 1                  (default to 1)
   Else
     Go to next record               (to bring up a new record)
     CustomerID = CustID + 1
   End If
   Move the cursor to the Title field  (save user an extra keystroke)
End Proc
```

Step 1: Using the wizard to place an Add Customer command button.

We can get off to a flying start by using a wizard to create some of the **On Click** event code for the Add Customer button, automatically. Looking at the pseudocode, the first thing that the code needs to do is to go to the last record.

- Open the **frmCustomer** form in Design view.
- Make sure the Control Wizards tool is selected.
- Click the Command Button icon and then click in the form header, next to the combo box.
- In the Command Button wizard dialogue box, select **Record Navigation**, and **Go to Last Record**. Click **Next**.
- Enter **Add Customer** in the text box. Click **Next**.
- Name the button *AddCustomer*. Click **Finish**.

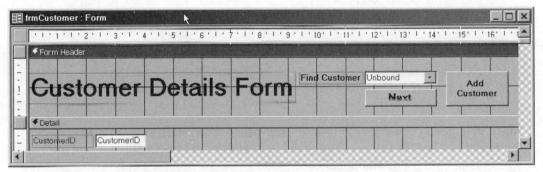

Figure 6.1: Placing the Add Customer command button

Step 2: Customising the code

- In Design view, open the Properties sheet for the **AddCustomer** button. Click in the **On Click** event property, and click the **Build** button (3 dots).
- The code that has been automatically generated will be shown (see Figure 6.2). It includes an error procedure to trap any errors and display a message if anything unexpected occurs. This part of the code can all be left as it stands.

  Access 2: The line
  ```
  DoCmd.GoToRecord,,acLast
  ```
  is replaced by
  ```
  DoCmd GoToRecord,,A_Last
  ```

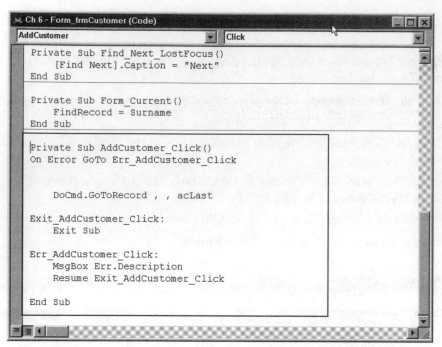

Figure 6.2: Code generated by the wizard (Access 2000)

- Make changes to the code, following your pseudocode. Remember to declare the variable **CustID** using a **Dim** statement, and to add comments to explain what's happening. The additional code is shown below in Figure 6.3.

Access 2: The changes to the code are shown below in bold.

```
Sub AddCustomer_Click ()

    Dim CustID As Long

    On Error GoTo Err_AddCustomer_Click

    DoCmd GoToRecord , , A_LAST
    CustID = CustomerID
    If CustID = 0 Then
        CustomerID = 1
    Else
        DoCmd GoToRecord , , A_NEXT
        CustomerID = CustID + 1
    End If
    Title.SetFocus

    Exit_AddCustomer_Click:
Exit Sub

Err_AddCustomer_Click:
    MsgBox Error$
    Resume Exit_AddCustomer_Click

End Sub
```

- Click the Compile tool to check for syntax errors (or **Debug, Compile**).
- Switch to Form View and test your code.

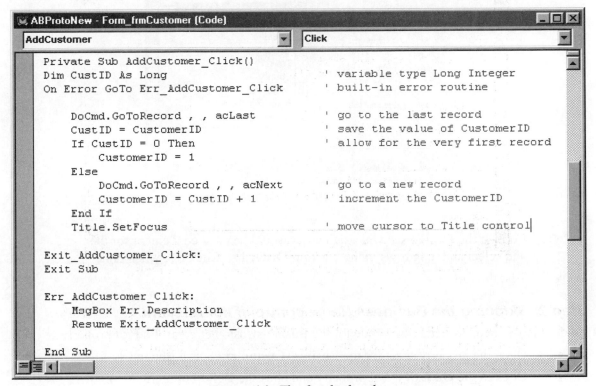

Figure 6.3: The finished code

Customising the form's tab order

In Form view, press **Add Customer** and tab through your form. Unless you have reset the Tab order, the cursor jumps all over the place. Two improvements can be made:

the tab order can be set so that the cursor goes through the form in a logical order;

the Business Name control can be skipped if Business Customer is not checked.

Step 1: Resetting the tab order

- Switch to Design view, and from the menu select **View, Tab Order**.
  Access 2: Select Edit, Tab Order
- In the dialogue box, select **Detail**.

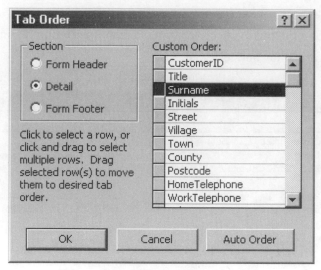

Figure 6.4: Altering the tab order

- Look at the form to see which tab order would be most convenient for the user, and select and drag rows in the **Custom Order** list. Click OK when done.

- Test the form.

Step 2: Skipping the Business Name control if not relevant

To do this you need to write some code for the BusinessCustomer control's Exit property.

- Open the property sheet for the **BusinessCustomer** control (the tick box).

- Click in the **On Exit** event property and click the **Build** button (3 dots).

- Select **Code Builder**.

- The code window opens. Enter the code shown in bold below:

```
Private Sub BusinessCustomer_Exit(Cancel As Integer)
'Skip the Business Name control if not a business customer
    If BusinessCustomer = True Then
            BusinessName.SetFocus
        Else
            CustomerNotes.SetFocus
    End If
End Sub
```

- It's always a good idea to compile your code to check the syntax. To do so, click the compile tool (or choose **Debug**, **Compile** from the menu). If nothing happens, then you have no syntax errors – though there may be logic errors which will come to light when you try to run the code.

  For example, suppose you have accidentally omitted the **End If**. When you compile the code, you'll get the following error message:

The compile tool

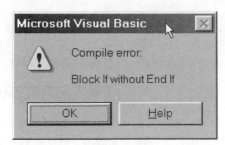

Figure 6.5: A compiler error message

- Close the code window when the code is free of syntax errors, return to Form View and try adding a new customer to test the BusinessCustomer control.

Setting default values in controls

You can speed up data entry by setting default values in controls wherever possible. In the **frmCustomer** form, we'll do two things to make data entry a little more convenient:

Change **Initials** and **Postcode** to uppercase, in case they were accidentally entered in lowercase

Let the **Town** default to *Ipswich*, and the **County** to *Suffolk*.

Step 1: Changing letters to uppercase

- In Design view, open the property sheet for the **Initials** control. Click in the **On Exit** property, and click the **Build** button.

- Click **Code Builder**.

- You need one of Visual Basic's built-in functions here, to convert a string to uppercase. There are several hundred functions and, if you aren't sure if a function exists to do what you want, you can use the Object Browser to look through them. Click the Object Browser icon now. (The icon may not be visible unless the code window is open.)

Object Browser icon

Access 2: In the main menu, select Help, Search. Enter Uppercase and click Show Topics. Then select UCase, UCase$ Function and click GoTo. Click Example.

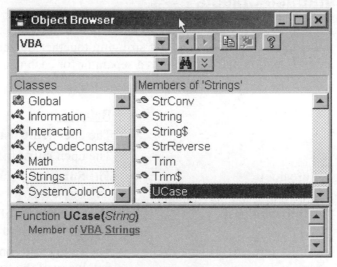

Figure 6.6: The Object Browser

- In the top left-hand box <<All Libraries>> select **VBA**.

  Access7: Select Library/Databases box, click 'VBA - Visual Basic for Applications'.

  Access 2: Skip this instruction

- Since you are looking for a string function, click **Strings**.

- Scroll down the Methods/Properties, and select **UCase**, which is the function you want, to show its syntax.

  Access 2: Skip this instruction

- Back in the code window, type the following code under the Sub heading:

  ```
  Private Sub Initials_Exit(Cancel As Integer)
  'Change Initials to uppercase
  Initials = UCase(Initials)
  ```

- Close the code window, and in a similar way, enter code in the **On Exit** event property for **PostCode**.

- Test your changes.

Step 2: *Setting a default value in a control*

- Open the property sheet for **Town**.

- We want to set the default value of Town to **Ipswich**. Which property should this code be attached to? **Before Update**, **After Update**, **On Entry**, **On Exit**? You have to be careful not to change an entry that the user has already made, back to **Ipswich**. In fact the property you need to attach the code to is a data property, not an event property.

- Find the **Default Value** data property, click in it and type = *"Ipswich"*.

- Similarly, set the default value for the county to *Suffolk*, if you did not already do so when building the prototype.

- Save and test your changes.

Referring to database objects

As you get more involved in coding, you will need to know how to refer to controls in forms and subforms. You write a complete identifier name by stringing together objects that contain other objects. Access uses an exclamation mark or a dot as a separator for each name.

Examples:

Identifier	**Refers to**
Forms![frmCustomer]	The open **frmCustomer** form
Reports![rptArtistName]	The open **rptArtistName** report
Forms![frmCustomer]![Surname]	The **Surname** control on the open **frmCustomer** form
Forms![frmJobSheet].Form![fsubItems]	The subform **fsubItems** of the **frmJobSheet** form
Forms![frmJobSheet].Form![fsubItems]![ItemType]	The **ItemType** control on the subform fsubItems of the frmJobSheet form

Forms![frmCustomer].[Caption]	The **Caption** property of the open **frmCustomer** form
Forms![frmCustomer]![Surname].[ForeColor]	The **ForeColor** property of the **Surname** control in the open **frmCustomer** form
Me![Surname]	The **Surname** control on the current open form

Notes:

♦ a dot is used as the separator when the next word is an Access-defined keyword like Form, Caption or ForeColor.

♦ an exclamation mark is used as the separator when the next word is user-defined like [frmCustomer].

♦ you don't strictly speaking need the square brackets round an identifier when the identifier is a single word like Surname, but you must use the brackets when the object name is more than one word, like [frmCustomer Details].

♦ a form is referred to using the name **Forms**, whereas a subform is referred to using the object name **Form** – a poor choice of keyword but we're stuck with it.

♦ a form must be open when code containing any reference to it is run.

♦ the keyword **Me** can be used to refer to the currently active form.

♦ you can get further information from the on-line Help by looking up **Naming Objects**.

Entering details of a new job

When a customer comes into the shop to buy a picture, or have a picture restored or framed, a job sheet is manually filled in. These job sheets are going to be entered into the computer at a later time – perhaps at the end of the day or week (an example of *batch processing*). You therefore have to think what would be the easiest way for this to be done.

Try to imagine the different situations which will arise. The user might:

♦ want to enter a job for a new customer;

♦ want to enter a job for an existing customer;

♦ not know whether the customer details are already in the database.

There are many different ways of tackling this problem, using Visual Basic modules. You could, for example:

1. open a new job sheet (**frmJobSheet**), and have a facility on the form to look up the customer surname, entering details automatically into the job sheet if the customer is already on file, or if not, asking the user if they want to enter customer details now. The customer form would then open for data entry and, when completed, control would return to the job sheet with customer details filled in.

   OR

2. open the **frmCustomer** form so that the correct customer can be located or details of a new customer entered and have a command button which will open a new job sheet with all the customer details filled in automatically.

The second approach has been selected in this project. When a new job is to be entered:

```
Open the frmCustomer form
Look up the Customer surname using the combo box and, if needed, the Next
button.
If the customer's details are not already on file Then
    Click the Add Customer button and add the details
End If

Click the AddJob button (still to be created)
(Try and anticipate any errors the user might make)
If Customer name has not been entered Then
    Display message "Please enter customer information before entering job"
Else
    Open the frmJobSheet form, showing the relevant customer details.
End If
When the job sheet has been entered, click a 'Return to Customer Details'
button (still to be created).
```

Step 1: Placing the Add Job command button

- Open the **frmCustomer** form in **Design** view.

- Make sure the Control Wizards tool is selected.

Control Wizards tool

- Click the Command Button tool.

- Click just under the **Add Customer** button in the form header.

Command button tool

- In the Command Button Wizard dialogue box, select **Form Operations**, **Open Form**. Click **Next**.

- Select **frmJobSheet** as the form you would like the command button to open. Click **Next**.

- Select the first option **Open the form and find specific data to display**. Click **Next**.

- Select **CustomerID** in both the **frmCustomer** form and the **frmJobSheet** form and click the **< - >** button in the middle (Figure 6.7). Click **Next**.

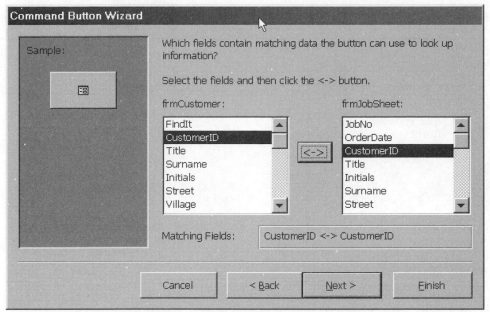

Figure 6.7: Linking Customer and Jobs

- Enter **Add Job** as the text to display. Click **Next**.
- Enter **AddJob** as the name of the button. Click **Finish**.
- Adjust the size and font on the button if required.

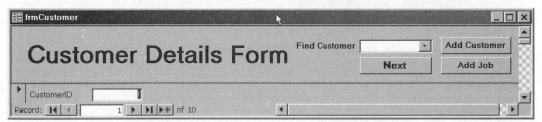

Figure 6.8: The new Add Job Command button

We now have to add code to display the error message *Please enter customer information before entering job* if the user attempts to add a job from a blank **frmCustomer** form. This code has to be attached to the **On Click** property of the **Add Job** button.

Step 2: Customise the Add Job button

- Click the **Add Job** button with the right hand mouse button.
- Choose the **Build Event** option from the popup menu. (This is an alternative way of opening the code window.) The code that was automatically created by the Command Button wizard appears as shown in Figure 6.9.

  Access 2: You will notice slight differences in the code.

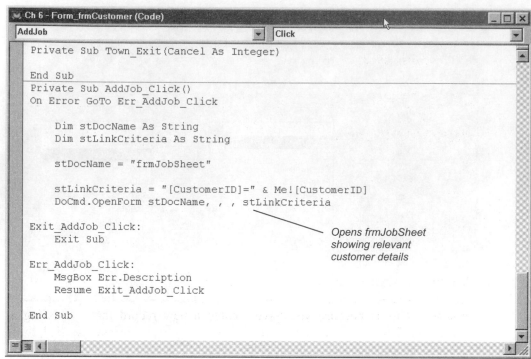

```
Ch 6 - Form_frmCustomer (Code)
AddJob                                    Click

Private Sub Town_Exit(Cancel As Integer)

End Sub
Private Sub AddJob_Click()
On Error GoTo Err_AddJob_Click

    Dim stDocName As String
    Dim stLinkCriteria As String

    stDocName = "frmJobSheet"

    stLinkCriteria = "[CustomerID]=" & Me![CustomerID]
    DoCmd.OpenForm stDocName, , , stLinkCriteria

Exit_AddJob_Click:
    Exit Sub

Err_AddJob_Click:
    MsgBox Err.Description
    Resume Exit_AddJob_Click

End Sub
```

*Opens frmJobSheet
showing relevant
customer details*

Figure 6.9: Code attached to the On Click property of the Add Job button

- Amend the lines of code under the second **Dim** statement:

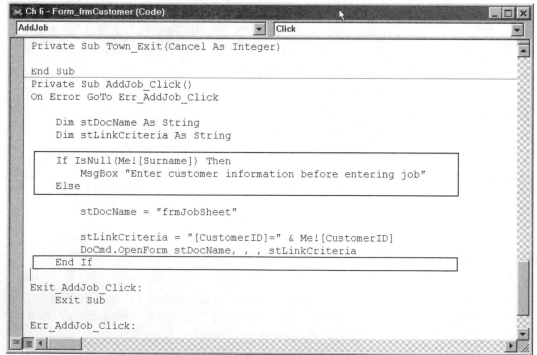

```
Ch 6 - Form_frmCustomer (Code)
AddJob                                    Click

Private Sub Town_Exit(Cancel As Integer)

End Sub
Private Sub AddJob_Click()
On Error GoTo Err_AddJob_Click

    Dim stDocName As String
    Dim stLinkCriteria As String

    If IsNull(Me![Surname]) Then
        MsgBox "Enter customer information before entering job"
    Else

        stDocName = "frmJobSheet"

        stLinkCriteria = "[CustomerID]=" & Me![CustomerID]
        DoCmd.OpenForm stDocName, , , stLinkCriteria
    End If

Exit_AddJob_Click:
    Exit Sub

Err_AddJob_Click:
```

Figure 6.10: The amended code (rest of code stays as is)

- Compile the code by clicking the Compile tool to make sure you have not made any syntax errors.

*Compile
tool*

- Save the code, close the window and switch to Form view.
- Go to a new record and then press the **Add Job** button. The following message should be displayed:

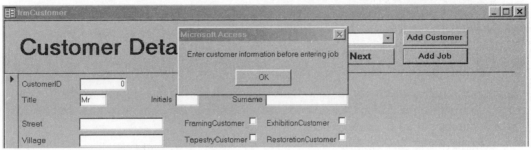

Figure 6.11: Displaying a customised error message

- Clear the message, go to a customer record and try again. If you try to return to a different record without filling in the **Surname** field, you may get an error message. This is because you have created a new record that is missing a compulsory field. To exit the record, type anything in the **Surname** field, then delete the whole record using **Edit**, **Delete Record** from the menu.

Customising the frmJobSheet form

When you display an existing customer's record on screen and press **Add Job**, **frmJobSheet** displays the first job for that customer. You can scroll through all the jobs for that customer until you open up a blank Job Sheet. If the customer has had no previous jobs, an empty form is displayed. Either way, the new blank Job Sheet does not display the customer name and address, which is what we want it to do. We have to add the code to do this.

Two questions need to be answered:

♦ what are the steps to be coded?

♦ what event(s) should the code be attached to?

We'll turn our attention next to the Job sheet form. We can attach most of the required code to the **On Open** property of this form. The pseudocode for the procedure is as follows:

```
Procedure OpenJobForm
   If frmCustomer form is open Then
      Go to the last job record for this customer
      If JobNo is not empty Then      (customer already has at least
                                       one job record)
         Go to the next record
      End If
      Make the CustomerID field in this form equal to the
            CustomerID field in the frmCustomer form
   Else
      Display a message "The Customer Details form must be open"
   End If
End Proc
```

Writing your own functions

Before writing the procedure **Open frmJobSheet**, we need to write a general function that will test whether a form is open, returning the value **True** if it is, and **False** otherwise. The function will be stored in a global module named **Misc**.

Step 1: Writing a general function

- In the database window, click the **Modules** tab.

- Click the **New** button.

Microsoft creates a new standard module and displays it in the module window. From here, you can enter Visual Basic code and create general functions and procedures which can be called from anywhere.

Access 2 is very similar.

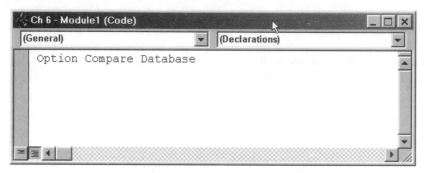

Figure 6.12: The module window

- Click the Insert Procedure tool on the toolbar (or select **Insert**, **Procedure**).

- Microsoft Access displays the Insert Procedure dialogue box, where you specify the name and type of the procedure you want to create.

- In the **Name** box, type *IsOpen*.

- In the type box, select the **Function** option. Click OK.

*Insert
Procedure
button*

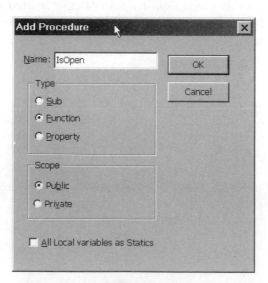

Figure 6.13: Naming the new function

Using SysCmd to test whether a form is open

Visual Basic and Access Basic include a useful function named **SysCmd** which can be used to return information about the state of a specified database object. It can be used to indicate whether the object (such as a form) is open, is a new object, or has been changed but not saved. The online Help gives a full explanation and examples of its use.

CurrentView is a Form property which has the following settings:

 0 if the form is displayed in Design view

 1 if the form is displayed in Form view

 2 if the form is displayed in Datasheet view.

Step 2: Test whether a form is open

- Type the following code (Access 2 code is shown below):

```
Public Function IsOpen(ByVal StrFormName As String) As Boolean
' Returns true if the specified form is open in form view

Const conDesignView = 0
Const conObjStateClosed = 0
IsOpen = False
If SysCmd(acSysCmdGetObjectState, acForm, StrFormName) <>
    conObjStateClosed Then
    If Forms(StrFormName).CurrentView <> conDesignView Then
        IsOpen = True
    End If
End If
End Function
```

> When continuing a line of code onto another line, put " _ " (space, underscore) at the end of the line.

(Note that you will have to replace the default function heading with the one shown above.)

Access 2: There is no Boolean data type, so Integer is used instead. Note that there are minor differences in the Access 2 code, shown in bold below.

```
Function IsOpen(ByVal StrFormName As String) As Integer
' Returns true if the specified form is open in form view

Const conDesignView = 0
Const conObjStateClosed = 0
IsOpen = 0
If SysCmd(SysCmd_GetObjectState, A_Form, StrFormName) <>
    conObjStateClosed Then
    If Forms(StrFormName).CurrentView <> conDesignView Then
        IsOpen = 1
    End If
End If
End Function
```

- Click the Compile tool to check for syntax errors.

- Close the module, saving it as *basMisc*.

Step 3: Adding code to the On Open form property

- Open the **frmJobSheet** form in **Design** view and click the **Form** box at the intersection of the ruler lines with the right-hand mouse button.

- Open the properties window and click the **Build** button to the right of the **On Open** event property.

- Enter the code shown below between the **Private Sub** and **End Sub** lines, each instruction on a single line: (There's no need to type the comments.)

```
Private Sub Form_Open(Cancel As Integer)
    If IsOpen("frmCustomer") Then
            DoCmd.GoToRecord , , acLast      ' go to last record
        If Not IsNull(Me![JobNo]) Then       ' if customer has a record
            DoCmd.GoToRecord , , acNext      ' open a new one
        End If
        Forms![frmJobSheet]![CustomerID] =Forms![frmCustomer]![CustomerID]
        JobNo.SetFocus
    Else                                     ' form is not open
        MsgBox "The Customer Details form must be open before you can
                enter a job"
        DoCmd.Close acForm, "frmJobSheet"
    End If
End Sub
```

> *Access 2: Enter the code shown below. Each instruction should be typed on a single line:*
>
> ```
> Private Sub Form_Open(Cancel As Integer)
>     If IsOpen("frmCustomer") Then
>       DoCmd GoToRecord , , A_Last
>         If Not IsNull(Me![JobNo]) Then
>             DoCmd GoToRecord , , A_Next
>         End If
>         Forms![frmJobSheet]![CustomerID] =
>             Forms![frmCustomer]![CustomerID]
>         JobNo.SetFocus
>     Else
>         MsgBox "The Customer Details form must be open before you can
>                                   enter a job"
>         DoCmd Close A_Form, "frmJobSheet"
>     End If
> End Sub
> ```

> *Remember to type this all on the same line, or type "_" at the end of the first line. What happens if you don't?*

- Compile the code by clicking the Compile tool (or **Debug**, **Compile** from the menu) to make sure you have not made any syntax errors.

- Save and close the code window, and test your code thoroughly.

Note: Closing frmJobSheet without entering a job saves a record with a JobNo of 0, and the next occasion will cause an error message about creating duplicate values. Press Esc first to delete the record. The form must be closed for the On Open event to be triggered.

Automatic calculations

The form still has several weaknesses, which your testing should bring to light. We'll address at least some of them. First of all we'll look at how to automatically calculate and enter the job value and the number of items in the job. Two functions will help here; **DSum** and **DCount**. Look up the details of usage and syntax in the on-line help.

It's a little difficult to decide which event to attach the code to, since we can't really anticipate what the user will do immediately after entering one or more items. One solution is to attach code to the JobValue's and the ItemsInJob's On Enter properties. The user will have to click in or tab into those fields for the calculations to be done.

Step 3: Automatic calculation of Job Value and Items in Job

- Open the **frmJobSheet** form in **Design** View, and open the property sheet for the **JobValue** control.
- Click the **On Enter** property, and click the **Build** button, then **Code Builder**.
- Type the following all on one line:

```
Forms![frmJobSheet]![JobValue] = DSum("[ItemValue]", "tblItem",
"[JobNo]=Forms![frmJobSheet]![JobNo]")
```

- Copy this line to the clipboard for use in a moment.
- Compile, save and close the code window
- Click the **ItemsInJob** control.
- In the **On Enter** property, click the **Build** button.
- Type the following all on one line (or paste and edit the line typed in above):

```
Forms![frmJobSheet]![ItemsInJob] = DCount("[ItemNo]", "tblItem",
"[JobNo]=Forms![frmJobSheet]![JobNo]")
```

- Compile, save and close the code window.
- Test your changes by opening the **frmJobSheet** from the **frmCustomer** form and entering a new job for an existing customer. Remember to click in **JobValue** and **ItemsInJob** after entering the item(s) to get them automatically calculated.

Step 4: Adding a form title and button to return to Customer Details form

- Switch to Design view.
- Drag the Form Header down to make room for a form title and the new control button.
- Use the Label tool to add the form title *Job Details Form* to the form.
- Adjust the font and size to your liking.
- Click the Command Button tool.
- Click next to the heading to place the Command button.
- In the first Wizard dialogue box, select **Form Operations**, **Close Form**. Click **Next**.
- Enter *Return to Customer Details* as the text to display on the button. Click **Next**.
- Name the button *ReturnToCustomer*. Click **Finish**.

Figure 6.14: Placing the Return to Customer Details button

Smartening up the fsubItem Subform

The design of the second project specifies that in the **fsubItem** Subform, a list box will be used for Item Type, so that the user just has to select from the list rather than typing in *Restoration*, *Framing* etc. When the user tabs out of the **ItemType** field, the relevant field on the **tblCustomer** table will be automatically updated – for example, if **ItemType** is set to **Restoration**, the field **RestorationCustomer** on the **tblCustomer** table will be set to **True**. It will also be necessary to 'Refresh' the open **frmCustomer** form to reflect any changes made in the **frmJobSheet** form, so that these are shown when the frmJobSheet form is closed.

Step 1: Creating a new table to hold item types

- In the Database window select **Tables**, **New**, **Design View**.
- The table needs only one field, **ItemType**. Leave it as a text field.
- Select the row and click the Key icon to make this the key field.
- Click the **Save** icon and name the table *tblItemType*.

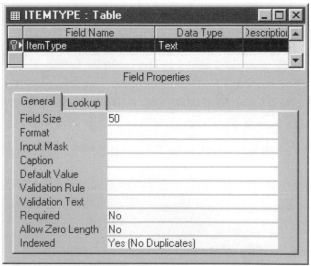

Figure 6.15: The tblItemType table

- Switch to **Table** view and enter 5 item types as shown in Figure 6.16.

Figure 6.16: Item Types

- Save and close the table.

Step 2: Make the ItemType control in the fsubItem subform a list box

- Open **frmJobSheet** in Form view.

  Access 7 & Access 2: Open frmJobSheet in Design view. Click outside the fsubItem subform to deselect it, then double-click the fsubItem subform to open it in Design view.

- Adjust the widths of the columns by placing the cursor between 2 columns (until the cursor changes to a different sort of arrow), then clicking and dragging.

  Access 7: Adjust field widths so that all fields are visible, as in Figure 6.17.

  Access 2: The form opens as shown in Figure 6.18. Adjusting field widths involves trial and error to make them fit the subform.

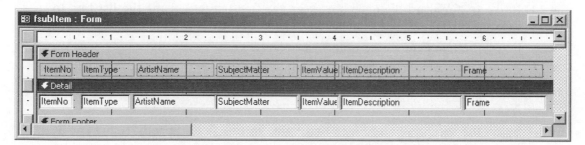

Figure 6.17: The fsubItem subform

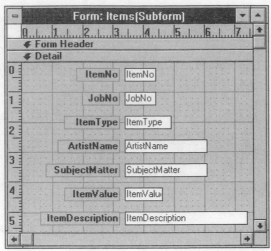

Figure 6.18: The Item subform as viewed in Access 2

- *Access 2000 only: switch to design view. You should be able to see all the fields in the fsubItem subform. If not, try closing the form and opening it in Design view. Enlarge the subform downwards to show the fields and labels.*

- Click the **ItemType** field and press the **Delete** key to delete the field, which is to be replaced by a list box control.

- Make sure the Control wizards tool is selected.

- Click the List Box tool, and then click in the space left by the deleted ItemType.

List Box tool

- In the first Wizard dialogue box, keep the first option **I want the list box to look up the values in a table or query**. Click **Next**.

- Select **tblItemType** as the table. Click **Next**.

- Click the arrow to move **ItemType** to the list of selected fields. Click **Next**.

- Adjust the width in the next dialogue box if you like, or leave it as it is. Click **Next**.

- Select the second option **Store that value in this field**. Specify **ItemType** as the field to store it in. Click **Next**.

- Give the list box the label *Item Type* and click **Finish**.

- The list box will appear in the **fsubItem** subform. You can click in its label and delete the characters.

- Click in the list box with the right mouse button and display its property sheet.

- Type *ItemType* in the **Name** property, and *ItemType* in the **Control Source** property.

- Set the **Tab Index** property to *1*, so that it will get the focus after the **ItemNo** control. All the other Tab index numbers will automatically adjust themselves.

- Save and close **fsubItems**.

- Save and close the **frmJobSheet**.

- Test the changes by opening the **frmCustomer** form, selecting a suitable customer and adding a new job. You can alter the field widths in the subform while in Form View so that they are all visible.

The next step is to make one of the fields in the Customer table automatically set to True – for example, if the **ItemType** is **Framing**, the **FramingCustomer** field in the **tblCustomer** table will be set to **True**, and so on. The code will be attached to the **On Exit** property of the **ItemType** control in the subform.

Step 3: Automatic update of a field in the tblCustomer table

- Open **fsubItems** in Design view.

- Open the property sheet for **ItemType**, and click the **On Exit** property. Click the **Build** button (3 dots), **Code Builder**.

- We are going to use the **Select Case** statement here. (You can look up details in the on-line help under *Selection Statements*.) Enter the code as shown in Figure 6.19.

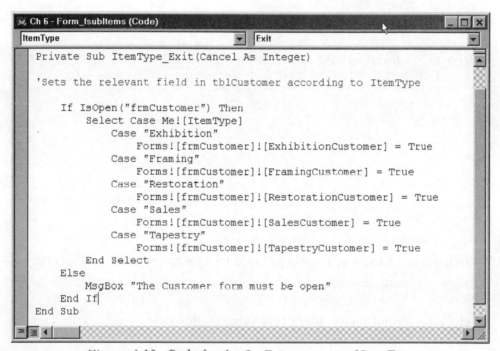

Figure 6.19: Code for the On Exit property of ItemType

Summary

In this chapter you have learned to:

- ◆ customise the tab order on a form and set default values in controls;
- ◆ use Visual Basic's built-in functions such as **UCase**, **Dsum** and **Dcount**;
- ◆ use the Object Browser to get more information on functions;
- ◆ use the correct syntax for referring to database objects;
- ◆ write general functions;
- ◆ use the **SysCmd** function to check on the state of a form;
- ◆ use the **Select..Case** statement;
- ◆ trap errors and display customised error messages;
- ◆ compile your code to check for syntax errors.

For online information about	**On the Help menu, search for**
Altering the tab order	*Tab order*
Object Browser	*Object Browser* then *Work with objects in Visual Basic for Applications using the Object Browser*
Syntax for naming objects	*Naming objects*
Displaying a message box	*Message box*
Select..case statement	*Conditional statements*
SysCmd	*SysCmd*

Chapter 7 – Helping the User to Look Up Information

Objectives

By the end of this chapter you will have learned how to:

write code to enable the user to look up all jobs for one customer;

use global variables;

test user actions and respond accordingly;

refresh a form so that it reflects changes made in another form.

Adding the facility to look up jobs

One of the user's requirements was to be able to quickly look up all the jobs for one customer. To do this, we can put a subform in the **frmCustomer** form showing **JobNo**, **ItemsInJob**, **Date**, **JobValue** and **Notes**. Then we can add code so that when the user double-clicks a Job Number, the **frmJobSheet** form for that job is opened.

Step 1: Creating a Jobs subform

- Close all open forms and from the Database window select **Forms**, **New**.
- Select **Autoform:Datasheet**. Select **tblJob** as the table where the object's data comes from.

  Access 2:

  a. *In the New Forms dialogue box, select tblJob as the table where the form's data comes from. Click Form Wizard.*

  b. *In the Form Wizards dialogue box, select Single-Column. Click OK.*

  c. *In the Tabular Form Wizard, click the double arrow to put all the available fields on the form. Click Next.*

  d. *Select Standard as the style for your form.*

  e. *Delete the default title and leave the title field blank. Click Finish.*

- The wizard creates the form and displays it on screen in Form view. Close the form, and when asked if you want to save it, click **Yes** and name it **fsubJobs**.
- Open the **frmCustomer** form in Design view. You may need to drag the footer section down to make room for the new subform, which will be placed under the rest of the data.
- You need to be able to see the database window as well as the frmCustomer form, with the new subform icon visible. Size and drag the **frmCustomer** form until you can see both windows. Alternatively, select Window from the main menu bar, and click **ABFrames:Database** to bring the database window to the top.

- Drag the **fsubJobs** icon onto the space you have made for the subform on the **frmCustomer** form.

- Click the subform with the right mouse button, display the property sheet and check that the **Link Child** fields and **Link Master** fields have both been set to **CustomerID**.

- Delete the field and label for **CustomerID**, and adjust the position of the other fields.

  Access 7: First click outside the subform, and then double-click the subform to show it in Design view.

  Access 2: Display the property sheet for the subform, and change the default view from Single Form to Datasheet. Save and close the subform.

- Switch to Form view and have a look at the form. You can adjust column widths to make the form look something like the one shown in Figure 7.1. If the settings for column widths change back to what they were when you close and open the form, then try opening **fsubJobs** in **Datasheet** view to adjust the column widths.

  Access 2: In order to adjust the field widths in the subform, it must be displayed in Datasheet view. (It should already be in this View.)

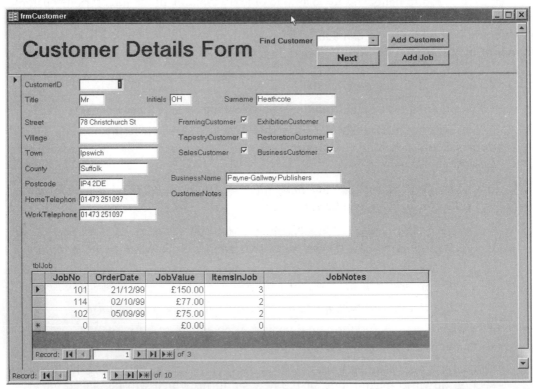

Figure 7.1: Placing the fsubJobs subform in the frmCustomer form

Using global variables

The idea is that when the user double-clicks the job number, the Job Sheet for that job will be displayed. However, we have already attached code to the **On Open** property of the **frmJobSheet**, which is executed when the user clicks the **Add Job** button. We want different code to execute when the frmJobSheet is opened by double-clicking the **JobNo** control in the subform. In this case, an existing job must be displayed, rather than a new job sheet.

We can get round this by setting a Boolean variable called **DisplayJob** to **True** when the user double-clicks **JobNo**. Then, in the code attached to the **On Open** property of the Job Sheet form, we can add an **If..Then..Else** statement so that one set of statements runs if the **Add Job** button click event caused the form to open, and another set of statements to run if the JobNo **On DblClick** event opened the form.

Up to now, all the variables used have been declared within the procedures they were used in. These are called procedure-level variables and their scope is the procedure in which they are declared. In other words, they are not recognised outside the procedure.

There are three scoping levels:

Procedure-level scope: variables are declared in the procedure and not recognised outside it

Private module-level scope: variables declared in the Declarations Section of a module as private

Public module-level scope: variables can be used throughout the database.

(For more detailed information, look up *Understanding Scope* in the On-line help.)

Since we want to pass a variable's value from one module to another, it has to be declared in a database module as a Public variable.

Step 2: Declaring public (global) variables

- Open the database window and click the **Module** tab. Select **basMisc**, and click **Design**.

- The code window opens. Enter the two lines of code shown in Figure 7.2 to declare two variables **DisplayJob** and **JobNum**.

  Access 2: The variable type Boolean does not exist, so Integer is used instead. Enter the following lines:

  ```
  Global DisplayJob as Integer
  Global JobNum as Long
  ```

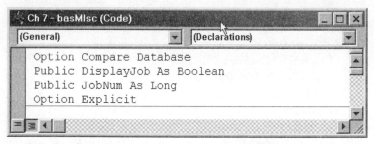

Figure 7.2: Declaring public variables in a standard module (Access 7)

- Close and save the module.

Step 3: Adding code to the On DblClick event

- Open **fsubJobs** in Design view.

- Click **JobNo** with the right mouse button to open its property sheet.

- Click the **On DblClick** event property, open the code window, and enter the code shown in Figure 7.3.

  Access 2: Enter the comments as shown in Figure 7.3, and then the three lines as follows:

  ```
  DisplayJob = 1
  JobNum = JobNo
  DoCmd OpenForm "frmJobSheet"
  ```

- Close and save the code window and subform.

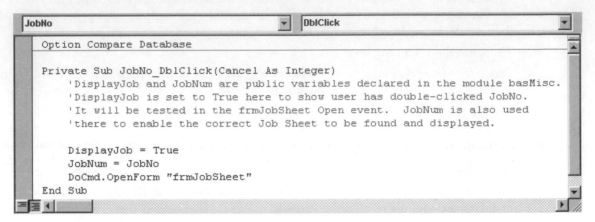

Figure 7.3: The On DblClick event code (Access 2000)

Step 4: Modifying the frmJobSheet On Open event code

- Open **frmJobSheet** in Design view and display the code window for the **On Open** event property.

- Amend the existing code as shown below: (new lines shown in bold)

  ```
  Private Sub Form_Open(Cancel As Integer)
      If IsOpen("frmCustomer") Then

          ' DisplayJob is set in the frmCustomer form to:
          ' - TRUE when a user double clicks JobNo in the fsubJobs
          ' - FALSE when the user clicks the AddJob button.

          If DisplayJob = False Then
              DoCmd.GoToRecord , , acLast
              If Not IsNull(Me![JobNo]) Then
                DoCmd.GoToRecord , , acNext
              End If
              Forms![frmJobSheet]![CustomerID] =
                    Forms![frmCustomer]![CustomerID]
          Else
          ' user wants to display a job whose number was stored in
          ' JobNum in the double-click event code in fsubJobs
          ' so look for that job and display it
              JobNo.SetFocus
              DoCmd.FindRecord jobNum
          End If
      Else
  ```

```
            MsgBox "The Customer Details form must be open before
                                         you can enter a job"
            DoCmd.Close acForm, "frmJobSheet"
        End If
End Sub
```

Access 2: Amend the code as follows: (new lines shown in bold)

```
    Sub Form_Open (Cancel As Integer)
        If IsOpen("frmCustomer") Then
        ' DisplayJob is set in the frmCustomer form to:
        ' - 1 when a user double clicks JobNo in fsubJobs
        ' - 0 when the user clicks the AddJob button.

            If DisplayJob = 0 Then
                DoCmd GoToRecord , , A_LAST
                If Not IsNull(Me![JobNo]) Then
                    DoCmd GoToRecord , , A_NEXT
                End If
                Forms![frmJobSheet]![CustomerID] =
                    Forms![frmCustomer]![CustomerID]
                JobNo.SetFocus
            Else
            ' user wants to display a job whose number was stored in
            ' JobNum in the double click event code in fsubJobs
            ' so look for that job and display it
                JobNo.SetFocus
                DoCmd FindRecord JobNum
            End If
        Else
            MsgBox "The Customer Details form must be open
                              before you can enter a job"
            DoCmd Close A_Form, "frmJobSheet"
        End If
    End Sub
```

```
Form                                    ▼  Open                                          ▼
  Private Sub Form_Open(Cancel As Integer)
    If IsOpen("frmCustomer") Then

    'DisplayJob is set in the frmCustomer form to :
    ' - TRUE when a user double-clicks JobNo in fsubJobs
    ' - FALSE when a user clicks the AddJob button

      If DisplayJob = False Then
          DoCmd.GoToRecord , , acLast
          If Not IsNull(Me![JobNo]) Then
              DoCmd.GoToRecord , , acNext
          End If
          Forms![frmJobSheet]![CustomerID] = Forms![frmCustomer]![CustomerID]
      Else
      ' user wants to display a job whose number was stored in
      ' JobNum by the double-click event code in fsubJobs
      ' so look for that job and display it
          JobNo.SetFocus
          DoCmd.FindRecord JobNum
      End If
    Else
        MsgBox "The Customer Details form must be open before you can enter a job"
        DoCmd.Close acForm, "frmJobSheet"
    End If
End Sub
```

Figure 7.4: frmJobSheet On Open event code

Step 5: Modify the Add Job code in the frmCustomer form

- Open the **frmCustomer** form in Design view, and click the **Add Job** button with the right mouse button to display the property sheet.

- Click the **On Click** event property, and click the **Build** button (3 dots).

- Amend the existing code by adding in the three lines shown in bold below:

```
Sub AddJob_Click()
On Error GoTo Err_AddJob_Click

    Dim stDocName As String
    Dim stLinkCriteria As String

    If IsNull(Me![Surname]) Then
        MsgBox "Enter customer information before entering job"
    Else
        'DisplayJob is a global variable defined in basMisc
        'and tested in frmJobSheet On Open
        DisplayJob = False
        stDocName = "frmJobSheet"

        stLinkCriteria = "[CustomerID]=" & Me![CustomerID]
        DoCmd.OpenForm stDocName, , , stLinkCriteria
    End If
Exit_AddJob_Click:
    Exit Sub
Err_AddJob_Click:
    MsgBox Err.Description
    Resume Exit_AddJob_Click
End Sub
```

Access 2: Instead of the statement

```
DisplayJob = False
```

type

```
DisplayJob = 0
```

The whole module is shown in Figure 7.5

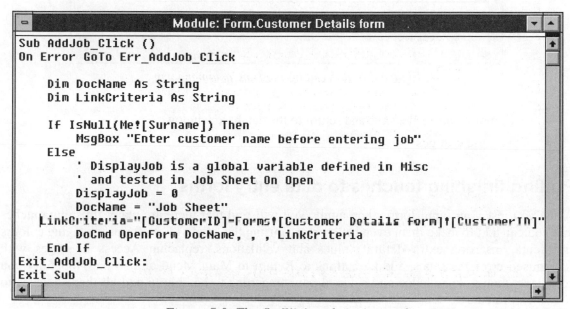

```
Module: Form.Customer Details form

Sub AddJob_Click ()
On Error GoTo Err_AddJob_Click

    Dim DocName As String
    Dim LinkCriteria As String

    If IsNull(Me![Surname]) Then
        MsgBox "Enter customer name before entering job"
    Else
        ' DisplayJob is a global variable defined in Misc
        ' and tested in Job Sheet On Open
        DisplayJob = 0
        DocName = "Job Sheet"
    LinkCriteria="[CustomerID]=Forms![Customer Details form]![CustomerID]"
        DoCmd OpenForm DocName, , , LinkCriteria
    End If
Exit_AddJob_Click:
Exit Sub
```

Figure 7.5: The OnClick code in Access 2

- Compile, save by clicking the disk icon, and close the code window
- Switch to Form view and test the **Add Job** button and the double-click on **JobNo** in the subform.

You may notice that when you add a new job, the new job is not shown in the subform when you return to the **frmCustomer** form. If you go to a different record, and then return to the original record, the new job will appear. We can add code to 'refresh' the current form so that the changes appear immediately in the current record.

The **Refresh** method tells Access to update the data displayed on the form with the current values from an underlying table.

Step 6: Refreshing the frmCustomer form when a new job is added

- Open the **frmJobSheet** in **Design** view and click the **Return to Customer Details** button with the right mouse button to display the property sheet.
- Click the **On Click** property, and click the **Build** button to open up the code window.
- Add the three lines of code shown below just before the **DoCmd.Close** command:

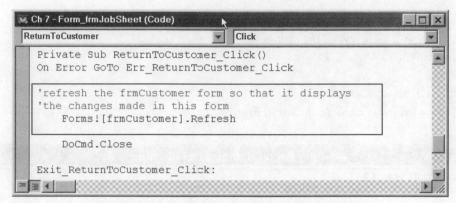

Figure 7.6: Refreshing the frmCustomer form

- Compile your code, save and return to the database window.
- Test the changes.

Putting finishing touches to data entry forms

When you test your input forms thoroughly, you will find that there are many finishing touches that you can add to make them even better: reorganising the layout of the forms, changing colours and fonts, inserting extra default values and validations, replacing Access messages with customised error messages, adding buttons to Return to Main Menu and so on. Hopefully you now have enough knowledge and skills at your fingertips to be able to add all these touches to your own project.

Try adding an event procedure to the **JobNo** field on **frmJobSheet** to display an error message if the user leaves the ID as 0 and then moves out of the field.

Summary

In this chapter you have used Visual Basic procedures to make the data entry forms as convenient as possible for the user. You have learned:

- ◆ how to declare and use global variables;
- ◆ how to update values in one form from another form;
- ◆ how to refresh a form to update the data displayed in the current form.

For online information about	On the Help menu, search for
Scope of variables	*understanding scope*
Refreshing a form with current values	*refresh*

Chapter 8 – Concentrating on Output

Objectives

By the end of this chapter you will have learned how to:

allow the user to specify a condition in a query;

perform the Mail Merge from Access;

make the Main Menu load automatically on start-up;

add a password.

Querying the database

In the last two chapters we have been concentrating on getting data IN to the database. Now we turn our attention to how to get the required information OUT of the database in a suitable format; for example, for on-screen viewing, printing in a report or sending letters to selected customers.

In the prototype, two queries were created and saved; **qryCustomerJob** which was used as the basis for the **frmJobSheet** form, and **qryBusinessCustomer**, used as the basis for the report of all Business Customers.

Several more queries have been created for the finished project; we'll go through the steps for creating the query designed to pick out all customers who have had jobs totalling more than a value specified by the user at run time. None of the other queries will use any new or different techniques.

Step 1: Creating the qryJobValue query

- From the Database window, click the **Queries** tab and select **New**. Do not use the Database wizard.

- In the Show Table dialogue box, add **tblCustomer** and **tblJob**. Close the dialogue box.

- Place the following fields in the table shown at the bottom of the screen by double-clicking them or dragging them:

  Title, Initials, Surname, Street, Village, Town, County, Postcode (from **tblCustomer**)

  CustomerID, JobValue (from **tblJob**)

- Click the **Totals** tool in the toolbar. This will make an extra **Total** row visible in the table.

Totals tool

- In the **JobValue** column, click the **Total** row and select **Sum**. This will automatically calculate the sum of all jobs for each customer.

- In the **Criteria** row of the **JobValue** column, enter

  >=[Please enter minimum total job value]

(The >= specifies that you are looking for customers whose job values are **greater than or equal to** the value entered when the query is executed.)

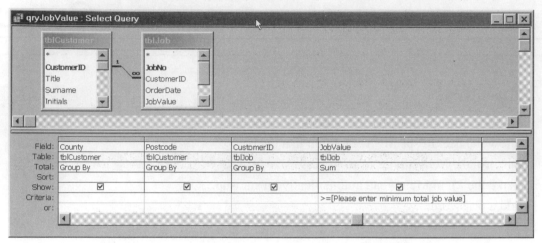

Figure 8.1: Entering a Sum function and variable criteria

Run tool

- Test the query by pressing the Run tool.

- A dialogue box will appear, asking you to enter a minimum value. Enter a suitable value.

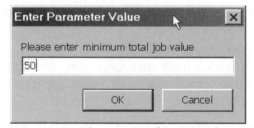

Figure 8.2: Allowing the user to specify a value

- Switch back to Design view. It would be better to sort the names by Surname and Initial. Click in the **Sort** row of **Initials**, and specify **Ascending**. Do the same in the **Surname** column.

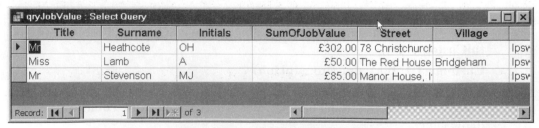

Figure 8.3: Query results

- Test your query again. It may not work quite correctly if the **Initials** field precedes the **Surname** field, because Initials is used as the first sort field rather than Surname. To correct this, you need to switch the two columns in the Query.

- In Design view, click just above the **Surname** column title to select the column. Then click again in the same spot, holding the mouse button down and dragging to the left of **Initials**.

- Test your query again and if all is well, save it, giving it the title *qryJobValue*.

Step 2: Creating a report from the query

Nothing new here; the report can be created using a wizard, and the fields moved around as required. The final report should look something like Figure 8.4.

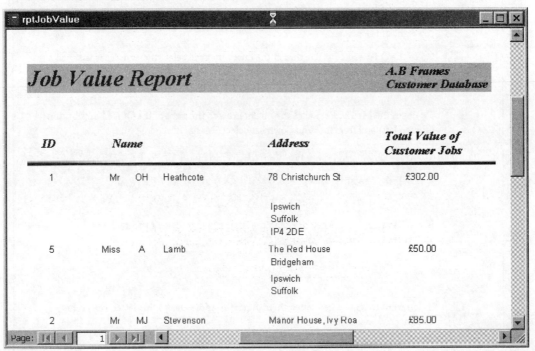

Figure 8.4: The rptJobValue report

Performing the mail merge

In Chapter 4 (Prototyping), we took a look at how to create a standard letter in Word, opened directly from Access using the OfficeLinks tool. For the finished application, a different letter will have to be created to match each set of customers for which a query has been created, since each letter uses a different data source. It is also possible that the users, once they become more confident in the use of the system, may want to create a completely new query and a standard letter to the new selection of customers.

In order to give them the flexibility to do this, but at the same time provide some guidance, the system design specifies that when the user selects the Mail Merge option from the menu, a form will open up with clear instructions displayed.

Step 1: Create a blank form with Mail Merge instructions

- From the database window, click the **Forms** tab and then click **New**.

- In the New Form dialogue box, select **Design View** and leave the table or query list box empty. Click OK. An empty form will be created. We are aiming to make it look something like Figure 8.5.

  Access 2: In the New Form dialogue box, select Blank Form.

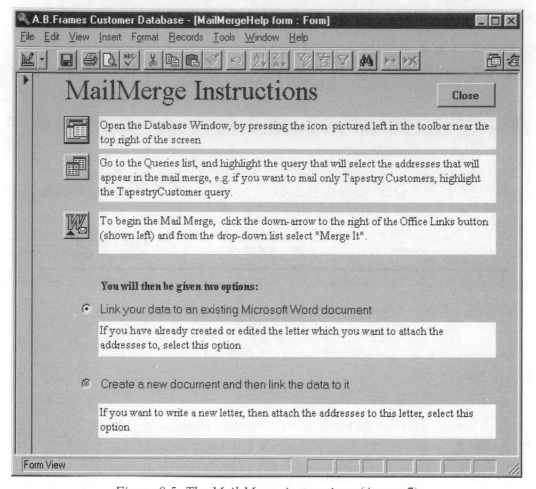

Figure 8.5: The Mail Merge instructions (Access 7)

- Place a heading on the form by clicking the Label tool and then clicking and dragging at the top of the form. Adjust type size and font as required.

- Make sure the Control Wizards tool is deselected and click the Command Button tool. Click in the form.

- Now put a picture of the database window tool on the button, by altering its Picture property. Click the button with the right mouse button to open its property sheet.

- Click the **Picture** property, then the **Build** button.

  Not in Access 2

- The complete list of bitmap images appears in the Picture Builder as shown in Figure 8.6. Select **Database Window**. Some of the icons may not be available, but this won't matter so long as the instructions are still clear.

  Access 2: The picture is different from the one shown in Figure 8.6.

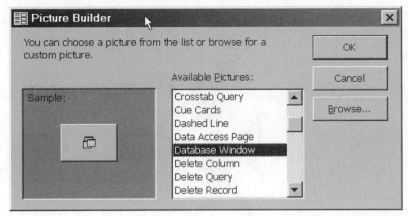

Figure 8.6: Placing a bitmap library picture on a command button.

- Finish off the form by placing text and buttons as required. The **Close** button is created using the Wizard, and simply closes the form.

- Test the instructions for the Mail Merge. You may find that a second version of Access is opened up. The only course of action after displaying or printing the letters is to close Word and Access and then start up again.

Making the Main Menu load automatically

You may like to automatically load the Main Menu or a title screen as soon as the user opens the database. You do this with the Startup command.

- Make sure you have created a Main Menu form, even if it just consists of a blank form with a heading "Main Menu".

- On the **Tools** menu, click **Startup**. The Startup dialogue box appears.

  Access 2: In the database window, select Macro, New. Select the OpenForm action and specify the Main Menu form. Name the macro Autoexec, and save it.

- In the **Display Form** box, click the dropdown arrow, and then select your Main Menu form (which you should have created in the prototype).

  Not in Access 2.

Next time you open your database, the Main Menu will appear automatically.

Note: The main menu for the final system is shown on page 3-16.It is different from the one originally specified for the prototype solution in Figure 3.6, page 1-27.

Adding a password

This is often impossible on a school or college network as it interferes with user privileges. On your computer at home, however, you can try it, though you should remove the password on any version you intend to use to demonstrate at your school or college.

- ◆ To set a password on the database, select **Tools**, **Security**.

- ◆ Click **Set Database Password**.

> **If you forget your password, you will never be able to edit or use your application again.**

Figure 8.7: A student who has forgotten his password and has to start his project again from scratch

Summary

This chapter has shown you how to put some finishing touches to an application. The sample project has been used as the vehicle for explaining techniques that you may be able to apply to your own project. It cannot be emphasised too strongly, however, that this book is not intended to be a complete Access tutorial, and that you should invest in one of the dozens of such books available on the market before tackling your own project.

Chapter 9 – Debugging Aids

Objectives

By the end of this chapter you will have learned how to:

monitor variables;

step through code a line at a time;

set a breakpoint to stop running code;

use a message box for debugging purposes.

Types of error

If you have done any programming, you will know that there are several types of error, including **syntax errors, logic errors** and **run-time errors**. When you write Visual Basic modules, you would be well advised to compile each module using the Compile button, which will point out any syntax errors in your statements right away. (It is not strictly necessary to compile the modules in this way, because Access will automatically do this before running a module, but it saves time to check the syntax and correct errors before attempting to run the code.)

The Compile tool

Run-time errors could be caused for example by not having a form open that is referred to in another module. Access displays an error message when this occurs and the cause is generally easy to trace.

Logic errors are the trickiest to find and correct, and Access provides a number of ways to help debug your code.

Using the Immediate window (called Debug window in Access 7)

When you have written a module and tested it, only to find it doesn't work, Access provides several ways for you to have a closer look at exactly what is going on. One way is to display the value of chosen controls or variables in the Immediate (Debug) window. To try this out, we'll use the code attached to the **On Open** event of the Job Sheet.

- Open the **frmCustomer** form in Form view and double-click a **JobNo** for one of the customers, which should open **frmJobSheet**, showing details of the selected job.

- Switch to Design view and click the right mouse button at the top left intersection of the ruler lines to display the popup menu. Select **Properties** to open the property sheet for the form.

- Click in the **On Open** event property and click the **Build** button (3 dots) to display the Module window.

- Select **Immediate Window** from the **View** menu at the top of the screen.

Access 7: In the Toolbar, click the Debug Window tool.

Debug Window tool

- Move the Immediate (it's easier to call it Debug) window to the lower right corner of the screen, out of the way of the code in the Module window.

- You can use the Immediate window to display the value of any control or variable. In the Immediate window, type

  ```
  ?DisplayJob
  ```

  and press Enter (see Figure 9.1)

- The value of the variable **DisplayJob** is displayed as **True**.

- Note that the question mark is shorthand for the Print statement; you could equally have typed

  ```
  Print DisplayJob
  ```

```
Form                                      ▼   Open                                          ▼
Private Sub Form_Open(Cancel As Integer)
   If IsOpen("frmCustomer") Then

   'DisplayJob is set in the frmCustomer form to :
   ' - TRUE when a user double clicks JobNo in fsubJobs
   ' - FALSE when a user clicks the AddJob button

      If DisplayJob = False Then
         DoCmd.GoToRecord , , acLast
         If Not IsNull(Me![JobNo]) Then
            DoCmd.GoToRecord , , acNext
         End If
         Forms![frmJobSheet]![CustomerID] = Forms![frmCustomer]![CustomerID]

      Else
      ' user wants to display a job whose number was stored in
      ' JobNum by the double-click event code in fsubJobs
      ' so look for that job and display it          ┌─Immediate──────────────[x]─┐
      ' MsgBox "JobNo and JobNum are currently " & JobNo & "  " & Jo│?DisplayJob          ▲│
         JobNo.SetFocus                              │True                  │
         DoCmd.FindRecord JobNum                     │                      │
      End If                                          │                      │
   Else                                               │                      │
      MsgBox "The Customer Details form must be open before you can│                      │
      DoCmd.Close acForm, "frmJobSheet"              │                      │
   End If                                             │                      │
End Sub                                               └◄│───────────────────►│─┘
```

Figure 9.1: The Immediate window (Access 2000)

Setting a breakpoint to stop running code

Sometimes it is helpful to watch your code running. You can do this by setting a breakpoint in the code so that when it runs in the normal way, it stops at the breakpoint and the module window is displayed.

- Place the cursor in the first line of the procedure:

  ```
  If IsOpen("frmCustomer") Then
  ```

- In the Toolbar, click the Breakpoint button, or alternatively, press the shortcut key F9. Both these are *toggles*, alternately setting and removing a breakpoint.

- Close the code window, and close the **frmJobSheet** form.

  Access 2: The breakpoint is cleared when the code window is closed. Therefore you must minimise, not close, the code window and frmJobSheet.

- In the **frmCustomer** form, double-click a **JobNo** to test the breakpoint in the **On Open** event of the **frmJobSheet**. The Module window opens, with the first

Breakpoint button

line of the procedure highlighted. The Debug window will still be open too, unless you closed it earlier.

Stepping through code line by line

You can now step through the code one line at a time, to see exactly what sequence the instructions are executed in.

- Select **Step Into** from the **Debug** menu.

  Access 7 & Access 2: Click the Step Into button, or press F8, or select Run, Step Into from the menu bar.

- Since the line just executed is a call to the function **IsOpen**, the next line to be executed is the first line of this function, so you will see the function displayed on your screen.

*Step Into
tool*

```
Public Function IsOpen(ByVal StrFormName As String) As Boolean
' Returns true if the specified form is open in form view
```

  Access 2: The next line to be executed is
```
Function IsOpen(ByVal StrFormName As String) As Integer
```

- Keep pressing the **Step Into** button (or the function key F8) and you will see one line at a time being executed. You can stop at any time and display the value of anything you want to examine, in the Debug window.

Stepping over procedures

Sometimes you don't want to bother stepping through functions such as **IsOpen** which are called by your own procedures. In that case, use the Step Over tool (or Shift-F8) instead of the Step Into tool.

- Close the Module window, leaving the breakpoint set.

  Access 2: Minimise the code window instead of closing it.

*Step Over
tool*

- You can't run the code attached to an event procedure except by causing the event to occur, so close **frmJobSheet** and once again double-click a job in the **frmCustomer** form – or you could press the **Add Job** button, which will also open the Job Sheet.

  Access 2: Make sure frmJobSheet is in Design view, and then minimise it.

- The module window will open. This time, select **Step Over** from the **Debug** menu.

  Access 7 & Access 2: Press the Step Over tool (or Shift-F8).

The code performs the function IsOpen without stepping through it a line at a time.

- Display the value **IsOpen("frmCustomer")** in the Debug window by typing
```
? IsOpen("frmCustomer")
```
  It should return **True**.

- Remove the breakpoint by clicking in the breakpoint line and pressing F9.

Using a message box to display variables

Sometimes it is convenient to know what values have been assigned to certain variables without actually opening the module window or the Debug window. One way of doing this is to insert an extra line of code in the module which will display a message box showing the variable you are interested in.

- Just before the line **JobNo.SetFocus**, add the following line of code:

```
MsgBox "JobNo and JobNum are currently " & JobNo &"   " & JobNum
```

- Save the code, close the **frmJobSheet** form, and test the message box by double-clicking a job number in the **frmCustomer** form. The message box is displayed as soon as the form opens, as shown in Figure 9.2.

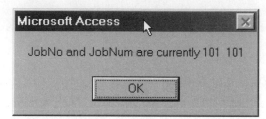

Figure 9.2: A temporary message box

- Click OK.
- Switch to design view, open the code window and delete the **MsgBox** instruction.

Summary

This chapter has covered some of the techniques you may find useful for debugging and monitoring your Visual Basic code.

Chapter 10 – Testing

Objectives

By the end of this chapter you will have learned:

the objectives of testing;

the steps involved in software testing;

how to draw up a test plan;

how to present the results of testing.

Testing objectives

Your test strategy should be included in the Design section of your report. In addition, your project should include a section on testing: the test data, the test plan, how it was carried out and what the results were. But what is the **purpose** of testing? It may seem obvious that it is to prove that the system works correctly.

In fact, you will formulate a much better test plan if you turn this idea on its head and consider the following rules proposed by Glen Myers in his book *The Art of Software Testing*.

1. **Testing is a process of executing a program with the intent of finding an error.**

2. **A good test case is one that has a high probability of finding an as yet undiscovered error.**

3. **A successful test is one that uncovers an as yet undiscovered error.**

In other words, it is not sufficient to think up a few tests which you are fairly sure will not make your program crash or give a wrong result; you must use tests and test data which have been carefully thought out to test all parts of the program. How many times does a lecturer spend only a few minutes testing a project before it does something unexpected, to baffled cries of 'It's never done that before...' from the crestfallen student! This should never happen with a properly tested system.

Designing a test plan

Your test strategy should be included in the Design section of your project. This means planning how you are going to ensure that each module works as it should, that the modules still work correctly when they are all put together, and that all parts of the system are present and giving the expected results for all valid and invalid input and under all conditions.

Typically you will start by adding several records at the prototype stage, and testing basic functions such as updating and deleting records, attempting to add invalid data and so on. Performing these tests will very likely give you more ideas for validations, and other improvements you can make to the system. Have a paper and pencil handy and jot these ideas down as well as the tests that you will need to perform to ensure that new modules and validations work correctly, and the expected results. These will then form part of your final test plan.

When the whole system is finished you will have to run through each of these tests again to make sure everything still works as expected. You would be surprised how often modules that worked perfectly last week no longer work, because of a change you have made elsewhere in the system.

Testing is a time-consuming, nit-picking business requiring much imagination and patience. Remember that you are trying to uncover errors, not cover them up.

Steps in software testing

1.   Module testing

As you complete each module of your program, it needs to be thoroughly tested. Even if you can't test every combination of paths, you can test the important paths, the extreme cases, valid and invalid data, and so on. For the purposes of your project, you should aim to demonstrate that you have tested systematically and that your testing is **reasonably** exhaustive. A maximum of 20 to 30 pages of actual test runs which cover major processes and show a variety of test data (i.e. extreme, correct, incorrect) is quite sufficient.

Remember to test:

♦   all computations in the module

♦   correct termination of all loops

♦   valid and invalid input data

♦   'exception' data which will make the module follow a different execution path.

2.   System testing

When all the modules have been written and the whole system put together, system testing can begin.

At this stage, you should ideally test your system with a realistic volume of data. If the system is designed to hold details of 5000 stock items, and you have never tested it with more than 8, there is no way of knowing how it will perform after installation unless you test it. Obviously, you will not have the time to enter 5000 different records, and the AQA recommendation is to enter about 50 records as a sufficient demonstration of a working system's ability to handle larger volumes of data.

Drawing up a test plan

The test plan should include a minimal set of test data and expected results for typical data and erroneous/extreme data.

For the module testing, draw up a test plan of preferably no more than two or three pages which shows that you have chosen your test data carefully, tested each module, and know what the results ought to be. A good test plan for the sample project can be seen at the end of the Design section in Part 3. The headings used are slightly different from those given in the blank form for your use at the end of the book – there is no single correct format so make your choice!

Test No	Test Data	Purpose	Expected Result	Comment /Verified
1	Enter incorrect password 'ABC'	Test password	Only password "ABF" accepted	
2	Enter CustomerID abc	Test invalid digits	Not accepted	

Sometimes it is impossible to show evidence that a test works correctly; in those cases, have your supervisor carry out the test and authenticate the result in the 'Comments/Verified' column. You could also use this column to reference the page number on which your test evidence is shown, or to make notes to yourself of any tests that did not work correctly.

Selecting tests for the test plan

Try to choose tests that test the more complex aspects of your system, such as calculations, command buttons that perform updating or open up a form with data already in it, and so on. Masses of tests for really trivial validations that are performed automatically by Access (such as a date in the correct format) are fairly pointless.

You may well have to amend or add to your initial test plan as the program develops, but you will find it very helpful to have a written plan at all stages, even if you keep adjusting it.

Similarly, if you design your system tests **before** you start coding, you will be forced to think about how this phase will be carried out, what will have to be done to make system testing possible, and how to ensure that it will be successful. The earlier you can foresee any problems, the easier they will be to solve.

Presenting the test results

Your test results should be presented in an Appendix, and cross-referenced to your test plan. They will normally take the form of test runs, screen dumps and file dumps. You may need to explain exactly what data was input. Use a highlighter pen to emphasise the key point about a screenshot, and annotate the output by hand to show what the test proves. Be selective, and consider it a challenge to make it as easy as possible for a reader to confirm that test results were as expected. As a general rule, include the absolute minimum essential to get the point across.

Test runs and screenshots with no annotation and no cross-referencing to the test plan are virtually useless!

For a large project with a correspondingly large number of tests, it would be sufficient to include samples of the test output and screenshots, and have the rest of the tests authenticated by your supervisor. There is no need to include hundreds of pages of screenshots.

Summary

This chapter has covered:

♦ how to draw up a test plan;

♦ how to present your results.

Chapter 11 – The Report

Objectives

By the end of this chapter you will have learned how to document your project.
It should include:

- A title page;
- A table of contents;
- Sections on:

    Analysis

    Design

    Testing

    Systems maintenance (technical) manual

    User manual

    An appraisal of the project;
- Appendices showing for example:

    input documents

    annotated program listings

    test runs, annotated and cross-referenced to test plan.

Introduction

The report that you hand in at the end of your project contains all the evidence of the work you have done over the past few months. No matter how careful your analysis, how appropriate the design, how clever the programming and how thorough the testing; if the written evidence is not there to prove it, you will not achieve a good mark.

It will take longer than you expect to complete the documentation. It will pay you to write the documentation in parallel with the other stages of the project and not leave it all to the end. Then, when you have finished the implementation and testing, you will be able to go through it all, proof reading, adding a table of contents, page numbers, and appendices.

Should the documentation be wordprocessed?

The short answer is YES. It should also be thoroughly spellchecked, both using the spellchecking facility provided by the wordprocessor, and by reading it through slowly and carefully. Remember that a spellchecker won't find misspellings like *the* instead of *then*, or even *curser* instead of *cursor*, as the manuals of one software firm will testify!

Wordprocessing skills

There are some crucial wordprocessing skills which you need to acquire in order to present a really professional-looking final report. This document must do justice to the effort you have so far put into your project; it is all that the examiner will see, and even if you feel you have perhaps not achieved as much as you could have, a well-presented report will help.

Use the Help system to learn new skills, including:

♦ **Setting styles for the various level of headings and text in your document.** (All the tips below apply to MS Word.) The **Normal** template comes with built-in styles for Heading 1, Heading 2, Heading 3 and Normal text. You may like to alter the font, size, style and justification of these, or set up new styles of your own.

♦ **Creating a Table of Contents.** If you have used styles consistently throughout your document, you can create a Table of Contents automatically. Put your cursor where you want the Table of Contents to appear, select **Insert**, **Index and Tables** from the menu and then **Table of Contents**. It can be updated at any time by selecting it and pressing F9.

♦ **Inserting headers and footers.** The project title and the page number can be placed in either a header or footer. Select **View**, **Header and Footer** from the menu bar.

♦ **Inserting a page break whenever you want one.** Press Ctrl-Enter.

♦ **Using numbered points and bullet points.** Use the tools on the toolbar.

♦ **Creating tab stops.** Never use the space bar to indent; nothing will line up when you print the document. Learn to use the tab stops on the ruler line, and the Tab key (above Caps Lock on the keyboard) to tab.

♦ **Inserting tables.** Use the **Table** menu.

♦ **Inserting screenshots.** When you want to take a screenshot to include in your User Manual, for example, press Alt-Print Screen to copy the current window to the clipboard. Then switch to your Word document and use **Edit**, **Paste**. A better way is to use a screen capture utility program to copy your screens to a file, from where they can be linked to your document using **Insert**, **Picture**, **From File**.

How long should the documentation be?

Basically, it will have to be as many pages as it takes to do the job properly. The AQA guidelines suggest that project reports should not exceed 4000 words, with listings and test runs being added as appendices.

The guideline of 4000 words is designed to give you an idea of the size and scope of project that is expected at this level. You must be selective in what you include and avoid duplicating information; if you have included a systems flowchart in the Design section, for example, there is no need to reproduce it in the Systems Maintenance section. Just refer the reader to the relevant page.

Putting it all together

Your project documentation should be neatly bound in such a manner that it can be read without a major unbinding job. A ring binder is too large and heavy to be conveniently posted, so investigate the shelves of W.H.Smith or any stationery shop to find something suitable.

Do not put each page (or several pages together) in a plastic sleeve; it makes the project report heavy, expensive to post, and inconvenient for marking.

The title page

The title page should include the title of the project, your name and centre, school or college. It could also include the date you submitted the project and your candidate number, if appropriate.

Table of contents

This is a must. Include in it the sections and numbered subsections, together with page numbers. Every page in your project should be numbered for easy reference; you can add page numbers by hand at the end to pages of test data, for example.

Analysis

A suggested framework for the Analysis section is given at the end of Chapter 2. Remember to include a write up of preparation for interview (such as a list of questions), and a summary of the main points gleaned during the interview. Do not include a transcript of the interview. A questionnaire, if you have used one, can be included together with a summary of responses. Your own observations of the current system, and deductions, are worth including also. If your analysis included reading about other similar systems, or trying out other similar software packages, for example, then that can be written up here.

Design

Headings for the design section are given at the beginning of Chapter 3. Look carefully at these and make sure you have covered all aspects of the design in your documentation. Your test strategy should be included in this section. You must aim to show that you have worked out what tests need to be performed and what results you expect. If you number the tests, it will make it easier to cross reference them to the actual test runs.

Testing

Testing is a vitally important part of the project. The test data and test plan should all be included in this section. The Testing Section should also contain a test plan analysis to show that it does test all parts of the system. Then, in the Systems Maintenance section, you can refer to any unusual results or unsolved problems.

Test runs may be included in an Appendix. **The test runs should be cross-referenced clearly to the test plan**, and be presented in such a way that the reader can see at once what a specific page of output is designed to show. Devising appropriate tests, organising and cross-referencing screen dumps and printed output can take a great deal of time and ingenuity. There is no point including several pages of output with no explanation of what test it relates to or how the output proves that a certain section of the program is working correctly. Make handwritten annotations on the output and use highlighter pen to show significant results.

There is a great temptation to skimp on this section of the project; the feeling is 'Right! I've finished the programming and I'm pretty sure it all works. Here's a disk – you try it...'. Unfortunately the devising and implementation of the test plan is your job, not the examiner's!

System maintenance

This section is aimed at a programmer who would be maintaining or enhancing the system. It could include the following:

1.   Schematic diagrams summarising how modules relate to each other (or a reference to diagrams already included in the design section).

2a.   Where a program or suite of programs has been written, for each module in the system:

        a brief description

        module name

        modules called up

        calling modules

        variables list – with type, purpose, format and example content

        high level pseudocode or flowchart.

2b.   Where a package has been used:

        a brief description of each object in the system, i.e. form, report, query, module.

        a summary of the purpose of each macro or module, and when it is used

        high level pseudocode or flowchart for each module

        an explanation of the features you have used, and a description of how you tailored the package to suit the user's requirements.

3.   Limitations of the system.

4.   Discussion of unresolved problems or odd test results.

5.   Special operational details.

6.   You will also be awarded marks in this section for program code, if your project has involved writing a program, macros, SQL or other code as part of the customisation of a software package. The listing should be a genuine printout rather than a wordprocessed document, and should be clearly annotated by hand wherever this helps to explain what is happening. It needs to be made easily understandable, for example by:

- using meaningful variable names
- stating the purpose of each variable unless it is self-explanatory
- using comments to state the purpose of each procedure
- using comments where necessary to explain the logic of a particular section
- grouping procedures in a logical order so that it is easy to find your way around a long program
- using indentation to clarify the extent of loops and condition statements
- using blank lines between procedures to separate them.

System-generated code such as that produced by wizards or recorded macros should be clearly labelled as such.

User manual

This section is aimed entirely at a non-technical user and should use ordinary English rather than 'computer-speak'. For example, do not say 'Boot up the system' when 'Switch on the computer' will achieve the same result.

Presentation is all-important here. Use whatever facilities your wordprocessor has to enhance the appearance of the document, spellcheck it carefully and read it through to make sure it flows well and makes sense. It should be a 'stand-alone' document and could even be bound separately from the rest of the project.

Your user manual should include:

- a table of contents
- an introduction, stating what the system is about and who it is for
- examples of actual screen displays such as menus, data input screens and output screens
- samples of printed output
- an explanation of what each option on a menu does
- any special instructions on how to input data – for example the format of a date field, or the range of accepted values in an amount field
- an explanation of any manual procedures such as batching or recording data manually
- error messages that may be displayed and what to do in that event
- error recovery procedures – for example what to do if you realise you have made a wrong data entry, or the power goes off in the middle of an update
- perhaps a hotline help number

If you have used a package, explain how to use the system you have created, rather than explaining how to use the software package in general terms. It is a good idea to test out your user manual on the user or a colleague to see if they can follow your instructions without any extra help from you.

Appraisal

Finally, your documentation should include a critical appraisal of the completed project. This should be clearly related to the list of specific objectives written in the Analysis section. The more clearly you have stated the objectives, the easier it will be to evaluate how well your system achieved them.

If the project has been written for a real user, it is a good idea to include the user's comments in this section, perhaps in the form of a letter written on official headed paper and signed by the user. If any suggestions have been made for amendment or improvement, include these as well, whether or not you have managed to incorporate the suggestions. Add your own suggestions for improvement and possibilities for future development. Do take note that a fake letter from your best friend or a glowing letter from an uncritical parent stating how marvellous your system is, flying in the face of all the evidence, is not likely to gain you any marks.

Be honest about the shortcomings of the project; if it is not complete, maybe this is because it was over-ambitious and you should say so. You will not, however, score many marks for criticising the hardware, software, staff or lack of time. One of the skills to be learned in writing a project is to finish it on time in spite of all the difficulties you may encounter!

Summary

This chapter has covered the documentation of a computer project. You should now look at the documentation of the specimen projects in Parts 2 and 3 for an illustration of the points made.

Part 2

Specimen Project (Grade D)

A.B Frames

Customer Database

Submitted by:

D. Student (Candidate Number 12345)

Any College (Centre Number 67890)

March 2000

Table of Contents

Table of Contents 3
Section 1 - Analysis 4
    1.   Introduction 4
    2.   The investigation 4
    3.   Objectives of the new system 5
    4.   Constraints and Limitations.. 6
    5.   Consideration of possible solutions.. 6
Section 2 - Design 8
    1.   Database Design 8
    2.   Definition of data requirements... 8
    3.   Method of data capture 10
    4.   Report design... 11
    5.   Menu design 11
    6.   Security.. 12
    7.   Test strategy 12
Section 3 - Testing... 14
    1.   Test plan 14
    2.   Test results... 15
Section 4 - System Maintenance 17
    1.   Software package.. 17
    2.   Tables 17
    3.   Relationships 18
    4.   Forms... 18
Section 5 - User Documentation.. 21
Section 6 - Appraisal 21

Section 1 - Analysis

1. Introduction

A.B.Frames is a small privately run business owned and run by Mr and Mrs Daniels. They specialise in selling pictures and restoring and framing pictures, photographs, tapestries and so on. They have built up a large customer base and this is increasing every year.

To cope with the increased number of customers and to keep track of what jobs customers have ordered in the past, Mrs Daniels thought it would be a good idea to have a system of keeping records of customers names, addresses and jobs and their interests (particular artists, exhibitions, tapestry etc.)

At present there are records of customers kept on a DOS system on a fairly old computer but no computer records of customer orders, so it is all reliant on memory.

So Mrs Daniels would find that if this information was put onto computer it would be very useful.

2. The investigation

Preparing for the interview

Prepare carefully for an interview with the user

In order to find out exactly what Mrs Daniels wants her computerised system to look like and how she would like it to work I have arranged an interview with her so I can ask her some questions. Below is a list of the main questions that I plan to ask her in the interview.

1. How many customers do you have at the moment?
2. Approximately how many new customers do you get each year?
3. At present what information do you keep on each customer and what new categories would you like to be on the new customer information?
4. What information do you need to know about each job?
5. What software packages do you have at the moment on your P.C.?
6. What type of printer do you have?
7. Do you have any preference what program the system is put onto?
8. What are the problems with the current system?
9. What outputs do you wish to obtain from the system?

Summary of the interview

After the interview I had a better idea of what is needed. At present there are about 500 customers, and about 30 new customers every year. The information that needs to be held about each customer is name and address, Business name if they are a business customer, and their particular interests (tapestry, framing, exhibitions etc.) The information that needs to be held about each job is the job number and date, the name and address of the customer, and the total job value. There could be several items on each job.

The Daniels have recently bought a new PC with Windows 98 and Access 2000, and they would like the system implemented in Access. They also have a laser printer.

Problems with the current system

Each time a customer comes in to buy something or have a painting framed or restored, a job sheet is completed. The customer is given one copy, and the other copy is filed. (Note: see Part 1, Figure 2.1 for sample job sheet.)

Frequently, a customer will come back several months later and ask, for example, for another tapestry to be framed 'using the same sort of frame as last time'. This means a lengthy search through hundreds of job sheets, and often the relevant one cannot be located.

The owners would also like some means of identifying which customers are interested in particular artists or subject matter (e.g. dogs, landscapes, portraits), who are their best customers in terms of jobs or amount spent, which customers are business customers and so on, so that letters can be sent out inviting selected customers to special events, sales or exhibitions.

Mr and Mrs Daniels are finding it very hard to learn how to use Access and set up their own database, and have asked for a customised database application to be created. They would like to learn more about Access and Word themselves so that they could for example create a new letter to be sent to a selected set of customers.

3. Objectives of the new system

1. The new system is required to provide the following information:

- a list of all business customers

- a list of all customers whose total jobs exceed a given value

- a list of all customers interested in a given artist or given subject matter.

2. It should also be possible to send a standard letter to selected customers, using criteria mentioned above.

3. It should be easy to look up the jobs that a customer has had in the past.

4. It should be easy to change things, e.g. add and delete data that is on the system.

4. Constraints and Limitations

Hardware

The hardware requirements should be more detailed

The system for A.B.Frames must operate on a PC with a laser printer.

Software

Specify the version number of the software package you and/or the user will be using

Mrs Daniels currently has these programs on her computer: Windows 98, Access, Word and Excel.

5. Consideration of possible solutions

A database would seem ideal for implementing the system for A.B.Frames, and as Mrs Daniels has requested that it be done in Access 2000 this is the package that must be used. It would probably be possible to implement the system using Visual Basic or another programming language but it would take a lot longer and would involve the owners having to buy more software which is not really necessary, as Access has all the capabilities required.

Using this package it will be possible to

• set up the necessary tables and relationships

• produce customised input screens

• design reports as needed

• make and save queries to select certain customers for a mail merge

implement a customised menu system

Assessment

This project involves the candidate in addressing and reporting on a problem associated with a real user. There is evidence of investigation, and constraints on the hardware and software to be used have been identified, albeit somewhat briefly.

Some objectives have been ascertained and clearly stated, although it seems likely that the interview may not have probed deep enough into the details of the user's requirements. Further evidence may come to light in the Design Section.

This analysis is extremely standard, written to a formula - it is in fact copied almost verbatim from a project report written by a student on a totally different topic, with minor changes in names and requirements.

It is best to avoid the use of 'I' in a formal report; try to rephrase sentences such as 'After the interview I had a better idea of what is needed' and write, for example, 'An interview was conducted to establish exactly what was needed.'

The choice of Access to implement the system has been satisfactorily justified both on the grounds that this is a package the users have already purchased and would like to use, and on the grounds that it is very suitable for this system and has all the required facilities.

Mark: Performance level 2: 6 out of 12. (Some analysis but limited in perception and scope.)

Section 2 - Design

1. Database Design

The database contains three entities, CUSTOMER, JOB and ITEM. These are related as follows:

An entity-relationship diagram such as this one is a must for a database project!

Tables will be created for each of these entities.

2. Definition of data requirements

The tables will contain the following data:

tblCustomer

You should specify the lengths of all the text fields

Attribute Name	Description	Data Type and length	Validation
CustomerID*		Long Integer	Unique primary key
Title		Text (4)	
Surname	Default "Mr"	Text (25)	
Initials		Text (3)	
Street		Text (30)	
Village		Text (30)	
Town	Default "Ipswich"	Text (30)	
County	Default "Suffolk"	Text (20)	
PostCode		Text (10)	
HomeTelephone		Text (15)	
WorkTelephone		Text (15)	
SalesCustomer		Yes/No	
FramingCustomer		Yes/No	
RestorationCustomer		Yes/No	
TapestryCustomer		Yes/No	
BusinessCustomer		Yes/No	
ExhibitionCustomer		Yes/No	
BusinessName		Text	
CustomerNotes		Memo	

tblJob

Attribute Name	Description	Data Type	Validation
JobNo*		Long Integer	Unique primary key
CustomerID		Long Integer	Must exist on Customer table
Orderdate		Date	Must be a valid date
JobValue	Total of individual item values	Currency	
ItemsInJob	The number of items on this Job sheet	Integer	
JobNotes		Memo	

tblItem

Attribute Name	Description	Data Type	Description/Validation
ItemNo*		Integer	Must be numeric
JobNo*	ItemNo and JobNo constitute the unique primary key	Long Integer	Must exist on JOB DETAILS table
ItemType		Text	Must be one of Sales, Framing, Exhibition, Tapestry or Restoration
ArtistName		Text	
SubjectMatter	Description of painting sold, e.g. Dogs, Portrait, Suffolk Landscape	Text	
ItemValue	Price charged for Sale/Job	Currency	
ItemDescription		Text	
Frame	Type and/or colour of frame	Text	

3. Method of data capture

Two data entry forms are needed.

1. Customer Details. The design for this form is shown below.

A screenshot smacks of 'post-implementation design' and is likely to be viewed with suspicion by an assessor!

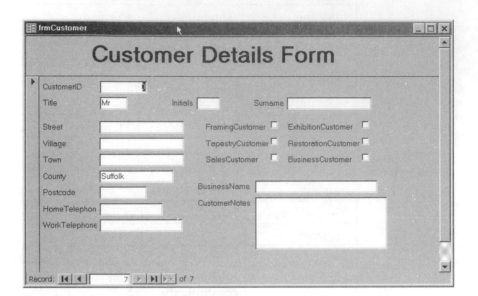

2. Job Details. The design is shown below:

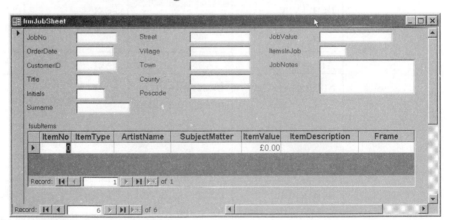

4. Report design

The format of the 3 reports will be similar. The layout of the rptBusinessCustomer report is shown below:

			A.B Frames Ltd Customer Database
Business Customer Report			
ID Name	Address	Home Telephone Work Telephone	
16 Mr D Grieves	19 Church St Ipswich Suffolk IP7 5GF	567890 453210	
576 Mrs P Mason	34 Kipling St Ipswich Suffolk IP6 4ER	745221 01728-998766	

Mailing labels will be created 3 up for standard size A4 paper. The standard letter will be created in Word.

5. Menu design

The menu structure is as follows:

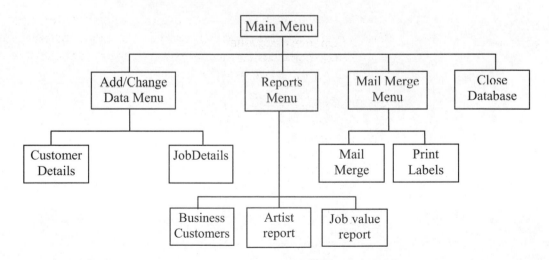

6. Security

A password will be attached to the database so that it is only accessible to someone who knows the password. Different access levels are not needed as Mr and Mrs Daniels are the only people who will be using the database.

7. Test strategy

This is insufficient for a description of a test strategy

The system will be tested using sufficient data to demonstrate its efficiency. All validations will be tested by attempting to enter invalid data.

All menu items will be tested, including input and reports.

The test data to be used is given in Appendix 1.

Assessment

The database has been correctly normalised, with three entities defined and the correct relationships between them specified. The data to be held has been suitably defined, and some validations specified.

The user interface design and the method of data entry are however, poor, and unlikely to satisfy the user's requirements. The following weaknesses can be identified:

- It will be up to the user to make sure that each customer is given a unique ID, presumably by first checking the last record on the tblCustomer table, and adding 1 to the ID to use for the new record.

- It will not be particularly easy to enter a new job. First of all the customer table will have to be checked to see whether the customer is already on file, possibly by using the built-in 'Find' option. The CustomerID will have to be noted, and then the frmJobSheet input form opened.

- On the frmJobSheet, mistakes could arise because the Job value and Number of items in Job are not calculated automatically, but have to be keyed in.

- In the fsubItems subform, Item, Artist and Subject Matter will have to be very carefully keyed in or the queries will not be successful; for example if the artist name is entered as 'Reynolds' in one record, 'J. Reynolds' in another and misspelt as 'Renolds' in a third record, only the first record will be selected. Combo boxes would avoid some of these problems.

- It will not be easy to look up past jobs for a particular customer.

The report layout for Business customers looks neat and shows the required information. Not enough detail is given on how the mail merge letters and the labels will be set up and printed. Does the user really need mailing labels? Would window envelopes be cheaper and easier? How will the users know who they have mailed?

The discussion on security is brief but satisfactory for this particular system.

The test strategy is weak. A test strategy should include different types of testing such as logical, functional and system testing.

Without planning to do any programming, it is difficult to achieve a really good system design and the end product is not likely to fulfill the user's requirements, even in this straightforward customer database.

Mark: Performance Level 2: 6 out of 12. (Evidence of design but lacking the necessary detail to produce a useable system without further development.)

Section 3 - Testing

1. Test plan

Test	Test data	Expected result
1	Test password with "abc"	Only "ABF" accepted
2	Enter CustomerID abc	Will not accept non-numeric value
3	Enter CustomerID 1 (see test data item 1)	Accepted
4	Enter a second customer with ID 1	Message displayed "Duplicate ID"
5	Enter job ID 101, for Customer 1	Accepted
6	Enter job ID 2 for customer 333	Will not accept non-existent customer
7	Enter Job with 1 item, type 'Framing'	Accepted
8	Enter job with 1 item type 'frming'	Not accepted; invalid type
9	Print report of all business customers	All business customers appear on report
10	Print rptArtist report, entering artist 'Constable' for artist name	2 customers should appear on report (Mr LP Heathcote and Mrs OH Head)
11	Print rptArtist report, entering artist 'Reynolds' for whom there are no jobs	Message displayed saying that there are no customers fitting this category
12	Print rptJobValue report, specifying job value of £50	All customers with over £50 in jobs appear on report
13	Select Mail merge option	Mail merge instructions appear
14	Select Print Labels option	Instructions for printing labels appear
15	Print labels for Business Customers	Labels printed for Ms James and Mrs Belles
16	Select Close Database	Access closes down

Avoid including too many trivial tests which simply test the capabilities of Access, e.g. Test 2

This is a very cursory discussion of test results!

The test results are shown below. The tests showed that the system does what it is supposed to do.

2. Test results

Test 1: test password

When the correct password was entered, the database opened. Otherwise, the following message was displayed:

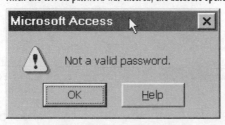

Test 2. Enter CustomerID abc.

Annotate the test output by hand to emphasise the purpose of the test and why the screenshot shows that the result was as expected.

Test 3 and 4: Enter CustomerID 1.

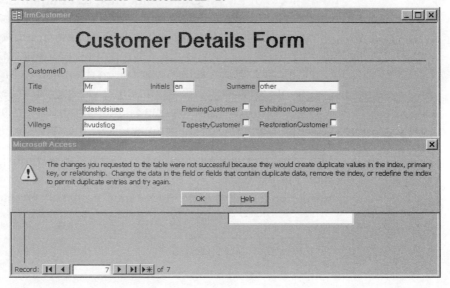

Test 10: Print rptArtist report

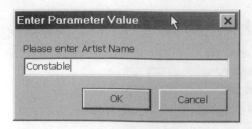

Test 15: Print labels for Business Customers

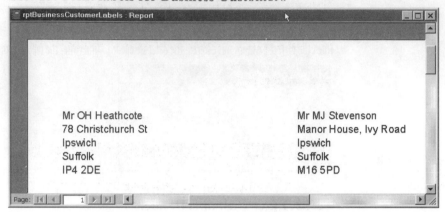

Your test results do not have to be word processed. You can include them all in an Appendix.

(In the project write-up, other tests would be shown as above)

Assessment

A good volume of test data has been used, sufficient to demonstrate all aspects of the program. Annotated test output has been shown for each test, but since the system itself is rather simplistic, many of the tests simply show the capabilities of Access in preventing the user from entering, for example, a wrong password or an invalid CustomerID. The tests have not been designed to highlight and correct weaknesses; for example in the report for Test 10, no Village was entered in the address, and so the report prints a blank line. Does it do the same on the mailing labels or the standard letter?

Mark: Performance Level 3: 3 out of 6. (A well designed test plan showing expected results supported by selected samples of carefully annotated and cross-referenced hard copy showing test runs.)

Section 4 - System Maintenance

1. Software package

This Customer Information system has been written in Access 2000, a database management system. It allows the developer to create a user friendly system with menus, forms and reports. Information can be stored, retrieved and printed. Access will answer questions by the use of a query, print mailing labels and standard letters.

2. Tables

Below are the tables in this database.

This section should show how you used the facilities of the package to customise an application, not how to use the basic functions of Access.

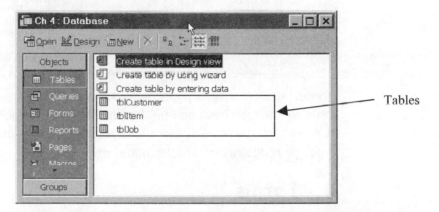

Tables

Tables must be set up at the beginning of the development process by selecting 'New'. Field names are entered, each field must be allocated a type (e.g. Text) and a size.

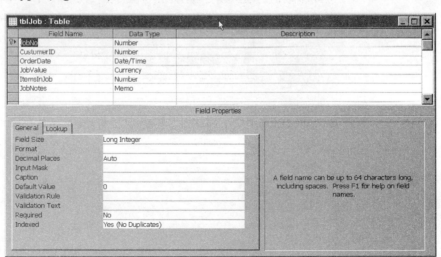

In the tblJob table shown, all the fields have types and sizes defined, at least one field must be the primary key, this field must always be unique to each record.

3. Relationships

Once all the tables have been set up they must be linked together by defining relationships. This is done by selecting the Relationships icon from the toolbar, or Tools, Relationships in the menu bar. Below are the relationships in this system.

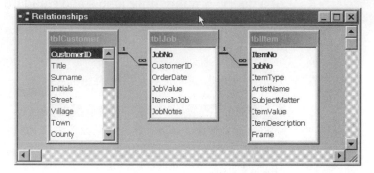

To define a relationship a primary key field must be dragged from one table to another they can only be linked by a common field such as 'CustomerID as the tblCustomer and tblJob tables are. There are two types of relationship 'one to many' or 'one to one'.

4. Forms

Forms are produced from tables or queries. Forms are where the data will be entered by the user in the fully functioning system. Below are the forms in the system.

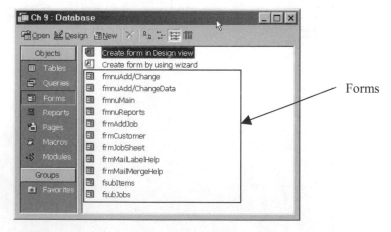

All the menus and Help forms are based on blank forms. The frmCustomer form, frmJobSheet form and fsubItem subform are based on tables.

To produce a form, 'New' must be selected then this window will appear:

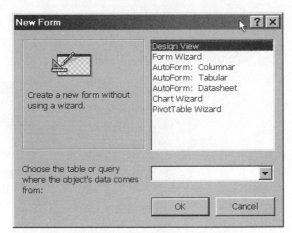

The form wizard will help you to produce the form step by step in a suitable layout. If the blank form is selected the developer must produce the form themselves by dragging all the required fields from a list which may take considerably longer, basically the wizard is a short cut and guide.

The forms in this system were customised in Design view using colours, different fonts, changing the position of the fields and editing the properties of the form. The design view of the customer form is shown below:

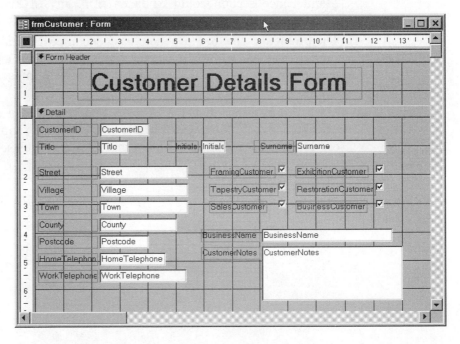

The fields and buttons can be moved anywhere by clicking on them and dragging them to the desired position. The colours are changed by selecting the palette button on the tool bar, the fonts and letter size can be changed by typing them in or selecting them from the two white boxes in the tool bar.

The properties list looks like this all the properties can be changed which will affect the layout of the form view or the facilities which are available such as editing.

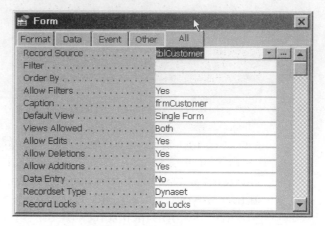

Assessment

This section should describe how the facilities within the package were used to tailor the solution to the user's needs. This should not be confused with a description of how to set up the basic tables, forms and reports using wizards, which is not specific to any particular system. The above Systems Maintenance section could be taken from any of hundreds of different projects with virtually no changes, and as such is of little value.

The problem is that because there has been almost no tailoring other than a minor rearrangement of fields on various input forms and reports, there is nothing to put into this section and it is therefore impossible to score high marks.

Mark: Performance Level 3: 2 out of 6. (Features used mentioned and "design views" of the candidate's own tailoring supplied. Samples of candidate's tailored features and/or macro listings with some annotation.)

Section 5 - User Documentation

(This section has not been included in the first specimen project. Assuming that it is on a par with the rest of the project with appropriate instructions and samples of screen displays, it could score a maximum of 2 out of 6 in Performance Level 2.)

Section 6 - Appraisal

The completed system was shown to Mrs Daniels at A.B. Frames and she was impressed. She found it simple to use and said all the facilities they need were included. A suggestion was made that a facility be included to display all the jobs for one customer. To do this another Customer form could be designed which includes a sub-form listing the jobs.

The system has met the objectives set in the analysis successfully.

These comments about data redundancy and referential integrity are quite meaningless!

- the system is very efficient and data redundancy has been reduced.

- the database contains all the required information and is easily added to but editing is a little more difficult because of referential integrity rules.

- the reports have been produced in the exact format specified and do what they are supposed to.

Future enhancements to the system:

- A macro could be introduced to automatically calculate the job value when several items of different values have been entered

- The mail shot could be further automated although Mrs Daniels is quite happy with this aspect of the system.

Oops! Read the report through as well as spell checking it...

I had many problems during development as I was learning more about Access as I went along. However I enjoyed completing this system and it gave me great satisfaction to overcome the problems and Finnish with a fully functioning user-friendly system.

Assessment

This appraisal is unconvincing; is there any evidence that Mrs Daniels is really as impressed as the writer claims? The shortcomings of the system are glossed over with only minor improvements suggested. The comments relating to the candidate's problems are not particularly revealing.

It is difficult to write a good appraisal, relating to the objectives, if the objectives themselves are not clearly and fully stated.

Mark: Performance Level 2: 1 out of 3. (Little attempt to relate achievement to the original objectives and/or shortcomings not identified).

Assessment of Technical solution

(The user manual gives a good picture of how the final system works, but the assessor will need to see a demonstration to assess the implementation, and will note down any good and bad points on the assessment sheet which is sent to the moderator.)

Various features of Access have been used to produce input forms, queries, reports, and a structured menu system. However there is a lack of attention to detail; for example the tab order on input forms is incorrectly set so that the focus jumps about on the screen instead of proceeding logically from one field to the next. There has been a heavy reliance on 'wizards', with some tailoring of forms and reports, but no programming of modules or macros to achieve an extra degree of automation which would remove some of the work from the user - for example automatically incrementing the CustomerID, or being able to automatically display all the jobs belonging to one customer.

The Mail Merge, which is such an important part of the user's requirements (as a means of keeping in touch with customers) is not automated, with the user having to do the Mail Merge from Word by creating the letter, selecting the appropriate data source and inserting the merge fields. Is this really what the user wants?

Mark: Performance Level 3: 7 out of 12. (Utilisation and development of features so that a fully tailored solution is produced i.e. the user does not have to use the raw package interface.)

Assessment of Quality of Communication

There are a few mistakes of grammar and spelling - e.g. 'Finnish' instead of 'finish' in the Appraisal, obviously put in by the spellchecker and not read through carefully enough! But in general the report is well written.

Mark: Performance Level 1: 3 out of 3. (Clearly and logically presented. Grammar, punctuation and spelling of an acceptable standard with few and minor errors.)

Overall grade

Overall grade for this project:				
	Analysis	6	out of	12
	Design	6	out of	12
	Technical solution	7	out of	12
	System Testing	3	out of	6
	System Maintenance	2	out of	6
	User Manual	2	out of	6
	Appraisal	1	out of	3
	Quality of Language	3	out of	3
Total		30 out of 60 = 50% (Grade D)		

Part 3

Specimen Project (Grade A)

A.B.Frames

Customer Database

A Level Computing Project

Submitted by:

A.Student (Candidate Number 543)

Any College (Centre Number 67890)

March 2000

Table of Contents

Section 1 - Analysis.. 4
   1. Introduction 4
   2. The investigation 4
   3. Problems with the current system.. 5
   4. Objectives of the new system 6
   5. Data flows... 7
   6. Constraints and limitations 8
   7. Consideration of possible solutions... 8
Section 2 - Design 10
   1. Overall system design... 10
   2. Database design 10
   3. Definition of data requirements 11
   4. Design of input forms 13
   5. Report design.. 15
   6. Mail merge 15
   7. Queries.. 16
   8   Menu design 16
   9. Systems flowchart 17
   10. Module design 18
   11. Security 19
   12. Test strategy 19
Section 3 - Testing.. 21
   1. Test plan 21
   2. Test results.. 24
Section 4 - System Maintenance 29
   1. System overview 29
   2. Tables and Relationships 29
   3. Forms.. 29
   3. Queries.. 30
   4. Reports.. 30
   5. Mail merge letters 30
   6. Macros and general modules 31
   7. Discussion of test results 31
Section 5 - User Documentation 33
Section 6 - Appraisal 33
User Manual 37
   Introduction 39
   Initial Set-up 39
   Menu options... 39
   Entering Customers and Jobs 40
   Looking up Customer Details... 42
   Reports 43
   Printing a report.. 45
   Mail Merge 45
   Backing Up the System 48
   Restoring from Backup Disks... 49
Appendix 1: Test Data... 50
Appendix 2: Module Listings 54

Create and use styles for section and paragraph headings. Then you will be able to automatically generate a table of contents. 12pt Times Roman, used in this report, is a good choice for body text.

Section 1 - Analysis

1. Introduction

A.B.Frames is a small privately-run business owned and run by Mr and Mrs Daniels. They specialise in selling works of art such as paintings and prints by local artists, and restoring and framing pictures, photographs, tapestries and so on. They have built up a large customer base and this is increasing every year.

Sales are boosted by holding regular exhibitions of paintings by various artists to which regular customers are invited as well as being advertised locally. Although the Daniels do hold a list of customers on a DOS-based filing system, they have no means of targetting customers who are likely to be interested in a particular exhibition, and automatically sending them invitations.

Mr and Mrs Daniels have decided to invest in a comprehensive customer information system to hold details of who their customers are, what orders or purchases they have made in the past, what their particular interests are and whether they attend exhibitions, so that they can offer their customers a better and more personalised service, save money on unproductive mailshots to the wrong customers, and boost sales by sending details of special offers, exhibitions etc. to carefully selected customers.

You must include an introduction. Background information about the business or organisation can be described if relevant. Then give an overview of what the project is about.

2. The investigation

Preparing for the interview

An interview with Mrs Daniels was arranged and a list of topics for discussion drawn up prior to the interview. These included:

- the precise objectives of the new system.
- the problems or weaknesses in the current DOS system and the manual system.
- the methods currently used to record data.
- the information that needs to be kept on each customer.
- the required output.
- the volume of data (e.g. number of existing customers, number of new customers each month/year).
- any hardware or software constraints - e.g. did they already have hardware or software which they proposed to use.

Summary of the interview

You are not encouraged to include an actual transcript of the interview; just give a summary of the information you gained.

A number of weaknesses in the current manual system and DOS file system came to light during the interview, and some new objectives were stated. These are discussed below.

Mrs Daniels has recently purchased a Pentium PC running Windows 98 and a laser printer. She has also purchased, on the recommendation of a friend, the Microsoft Office suite including MS Access. Her original idea was that she should learn how to use Access and develop the system herself, but having spent some time with an Access textbook realised that the task is more complex than she at first realised and would be simply too time-consuming.

There are about 500 regular customers on the old DOS system, with about 30 new customers being added every year.

3. *Problems with the current system*

i) Tracing previous orders placed by a customer

In your project, include sample input and output documents from the current system in an Appendix.

Each time a customer comes in to buy something or have a painting framed or restored, a job sheet is completed. The customer is given one copy, and the other copy is filed. An example is shown in Part 1, Figure 2.1. Frequently, a customer will come back several months later and ask, for example, for another tapestry to be framed 'using the same sort of frame as last time'. This means a lengthy search through hundreds of job sheets, and often the relevant one cannot be located.

ii) Inability to send targetted mailshots

The current DOS filing system does not hold any details on customers' particular interests or what past purchases they have. Currently it is not possible to send out a mailshot only to selected customers, although labels can be printed to all customers in the database. With the number of customers increasing every year, this is impractical and expensive.

iii) Lack of information about customer base

There is a general lack of information about who the most frequent customers are, who has not made any purchases for the past few years, what the most popular items are, etc. Access to summarised information of this kind could be useful for planning future stock purchases, marketing campaigns and so on.

This is one of the most important paragraphs in the report! If you identify and state the objectives clearly, the design and appraisal will be very much easier.

4. *Objectives of the new system*

The objectives may be stated in both quantitative and qualitative terms.

1. It should take less than 30 seconds to establish whether a customer is already on file.

2. It should be possible to go directly from the Customer Details screen to the entry of a job for that customer, without having to re-enter the customer's name, etc.

3. Data entry should be as fast and easy as possible, particularly as there are several hundred existing customers and jobs to be entered when the system is first installed.

4. It should take less than one minute to trace any past job for a customer.

5. There must be provision for multi-item jobs; for example a job could consist of the **restoration** and **framing** of a picture.

6. The new system is required to provide the following information:

   - a list of all business customers

   - a list of all customers interested in a given artist or given subject matter, or who are classified as 'Tapestry', 'Restoration' 'Framing' or 'Exhibition' customers

   - a list of all customers whose total jobs exceed a given value.

7. It should be possible to send a standard letter to selected customers, using criteria mentioned above.

8. The user must be able to create new letters whenever needed and perform a mail merge to selected customers.

9. The main menu should be displayed automatically when the database is loaded, and the whole system should be menu-driven.

5. *Data flows*

A data flow diagram of the proposed system is shown below:

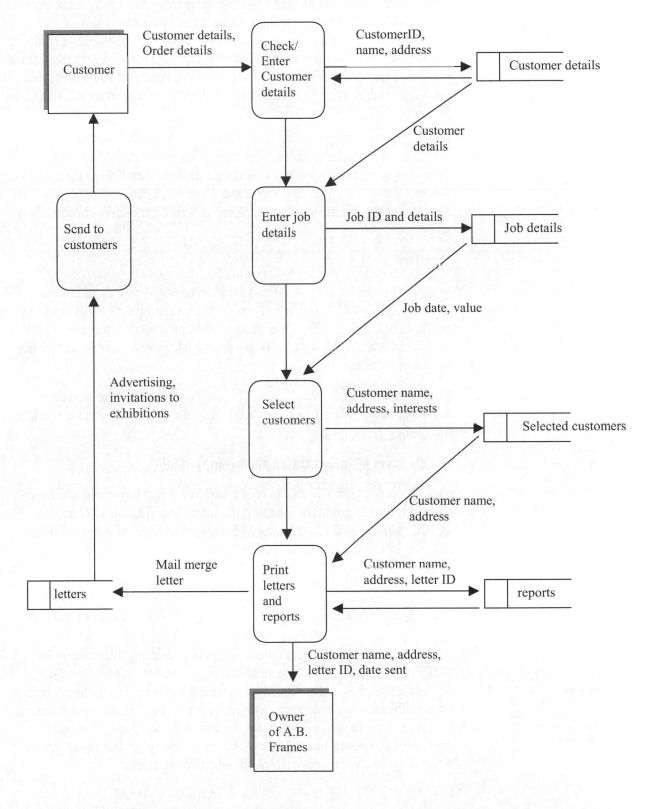

6. *Constraints and limitations*

System boundaries (scope of proposed system)

The system to be developed is a customer information system, and is intended to enhance rather than replace the current system of recording jobs. If this proves successful, it will be possible at a future date to replace the current method of recording jobs so that the details are typed directly into the computer and the required copies printed out. This could then be extended to link into a computerised accounts system.

Specify the details of the hardware and software that will be used both for development and by the user, including the Version number

Software

The customer has requested that the system be developed using MS Access 2000, so unless a good reason transpires for using an alternative program or package, Access will be the first choice of software.

Hardware

In order to run Access 2000 and be able to perform a mail merge using Word, a PC 486 or Pentium with a minimum of 8Mb, and preferably 16Mb, will be required. A fast processor such as a P120 will be needed if the system is not going to appear slow in switching between screens.

The user has a Pentium P200 with 16Mb, which will be perfectly suitable, and similar machines are available for development work at the College.

The user's I.T. skills may be a relevant factor in the design of the system

User's level of information technology skills

Mrs Daniels is familiar with Word and has good keyboard skills, so should have no problem entering data and learning how to use the system. She would like to improve her knowledge of Access so that she can in the future perform new queries and reports as the need arises.

7. *Consideration of possible solutions*

The AQA requires A level candidates to assess the feasibility of potential solutions and justify the chosen one.

A database package will be ideal for implementing the system for A.B.Frames, and as Mrs Daniels has requested that it be done in Access 2000 this is the package that must be used. It would probably be possible to implement the system using Visual Basic or another programming language but it would take a lot longer and would involve the owners having to buy more software which is not really necessary, as Access has all the capabilities required.

I already have some experience of Access 2000 and it is available both at home and at College for development.

Using this package it will be possible to

- set up the necessary tables and relationships

- produce customised input screens, using Visual Basic to automate data entry wherever possible and to perform various validations

- use Visual Basic modules to enable fast searches foe a particular customer and past jobs

- design reports as needed

- make and save queries to select certain customers for a mail merge

- link with MS Word to enable new letters to be composed and to perform mail merges to selected customers

- implement a customised menu system

Assessment

This project involves the candidate in addressing and reporting on a problem associated with a real user. There is evidence of investigation, and data flows have been ascertained. Constraints on the hardware and software to be used have been identified.

Objectives have been ascertained and clearly stated, although the project does not seem to be a particularly demanding one, being a fairly standard database type of problem. However scope for further development has been noted.

Mark: Performance level 4: 10 out of 12. (Extensive investigation of a demanding open-ended problem showing realistic appreciation of system requirements and demonstrating a high level of perception of a real user's needs. Clear and comprehensive set of measurable system objectives.)

Section 2 - Design

1. Overall system design

The input, processes, database tables and output are shown in the following system outline chart.

INPUT	PROCESSES

Customer Details:
    ID, Name, Address, Tel,
    Customer type, Business
    Customer (Y/N), Notes
 	
Job (Order) Details:
    JobNo, Customer ID,
    Order date, Order value,
    Number of items in job
 	
For each line of job order:
 	
    Item type (Sales, Framing
    etc), Artist name if picture,
    Description, Frame, Cost
	Add, edit, delete customers
	
	Add, edit, delete job orders
	
	Look up all jobs for a customer
	
	Print out reports:
	    All Business customers
	    Customers who have
	    purchased work by a
	    particular artist
	    Customers who have
	    attended exhibitions etc.
	
	Mail merge to selected customers

TABLES	**OUTPUT**

Customer table
 	
Job table
 	
Order Line (Job Item) table
	Display: Jobs for a customer
	
	Reports:
	    All Business customers
	    Customers who have
	    purchased work by a
	    particular artist
	    Customers who have
	    attended exhibitions etc.
	
	Mail merge letters

2. Database design

The database contains three entities, CUSTOMER, JOB and ITEM. These are related as follows:

An entity-relationship diagram such as this one is essential as part of the database design.

Tables will be created for each of these entities.

3. Definition of data requirements

The tables will contain the following data:

tblCustomer

Document the type and length of each attribute carefully, BEFORE you start work in Access. Discrepancies in the type and length of foreign key fields in different tables can cause major problems later on

Attribute Name	Comments	Data Type and Length	Validation
CustomerID*	Automatically incremented	Long Integer	Unique primary key
Title		Text (4)	
Surname		Text (25)	
Initials	Automatically converted to uppercase	Text (3)	
Street		Text (30)	
Village		Text (30)	
Town		Text (30)	Default to Ipswich
County		Text (20)	Default to Suffolk
PostCode	Automatically converted to uppercase	Text (10)	
HomeTelephone		Text (15)	
WorkTelephone		Text (20)	
SalesCustomer		Yes/No	
FramingCustomer		Yes/No	
RestorationCustomer		Yes/No	
TapestryCustomer		Yes/No	
ExhibitionCustomer		Yes/No	
BusinessCustomer		Yes/No	
BusinessName	Skipped if not Business Customer	Text	
CustomerNotes		Memo	

tblJob

Attribute Name	Comments	Data Type	Validation
JobNo*		Long Integer	Unique primary key
CustomerID		Integer	Must exist on tblCustomer table
Orderdate		Date	Must be a valid date
JobValue	Total of individual item values	Currency	(Automatically calculated)
ItemsInJob	The number of items on this Job sheet	Integer	(Automatically calculated)
JobNotes		Memo	

tblItem

Attribute Name	Comments	Data Type and length	Validation
ItemNo*	1,2 etc for items in Job	Long Integer	Must be numeric and unique
JobNo*	ItemNo and JobNo constitute the unique primary key	Integer	Must exist on tblJob table
ItemType	Will cause Check box on frmCustomer form to be automatically set	Text (11)	Must be one of Sales, Framing, Exhibition, Tapestry or Restoration (Selected from list box)
ArtistName		Text (20)	Selected from combo box
SubjectMatter	Description of painting sold, e.g. Dogs, Portrait, Suffolk Landscape	Text (20)	selected from combo box
ItemValue	Price charged for Sale/Job	Currency	
ItemDescription		Text (30)	
Frame	Type and/or colour of frame	Text (20)	

4. *Design of input forms*

Two data entry forms are needed.

1.   frmCustomer

This form will be used for several purposes so it needs facilities to

- check to see whether a customer is already on the database

- add a new customer

- move to the frmJobSheet form to enter a new job for the current customer

- look through all the existing jobs for the current customer and bring up more details if necessary

Look at any specimen input documents to see if certain default values would be appropriate.

Validations will be performed automatically. The CustomerID field will be an integer field and will automatically increment when a new customer is added, to ensure a unique ID without the user having to know what the last ID used was. Wherever possible default values will be inserted automatically (e.g. most customers are from Ipswich, Suffolk so the relevant fields will default to those values). Tab order will also be used to speed data entry; e.g. if Business Customer is not checked, the field for Business Name will be automatically skipped.

In order to look up details for a particular job, the Job Number field in the subform can be double-clicked to automatically bring up the Job Sheet.

The frmCustomer form will be as shown on the next page.

2.   frmJobSheet

This form will be accessible only from the frmCustomer form when the Add Job button is pressed, or a JobNo on the frmCustomer form is double-clicked as explained above.

The frmJobSheet form will be as shown on the next page.

CUSTOMER DETAILS FORM

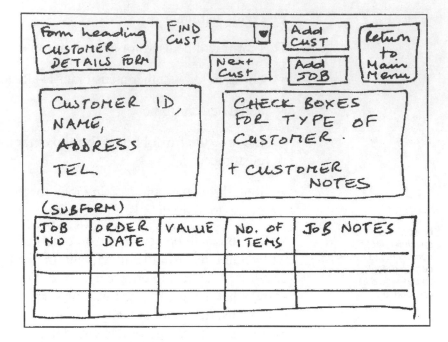

Hand-drawn screen layouts are preferable to screenshots of your final screens. These should be drawn BEFORE you start work at the computer

| Form heading CUSTOMER DETAILS FORM | FIND CUST [▼] | Add CUST | Return to Main Menu |
| | Next Cust | Add JOB | |

| CUSTOMER ID, NAME, ADDRESS TEL | CHECK BOXES FOR TYPE OF CUSTOMER. + CUSTOMER NOTES |

(SUBFORM)

JOB NO	ORDER DATE	VALUE	NO. OF ITEMS	JOB NOTES

JOB SHEET

Alternatively, you could print out the screen as produced automatically by a wizard, and annotate it by hand to show how you intend to customise it.

| FORM HEADING "JOB SHEET" | DELETE JOB | RETURN TO CUSTOMER DETAILS |

JOB ID [   ]   DATE [   ]

| CUSTOMER DETAILS (ALREADY DISPLAYED ON FORM) | JOB NOTES |

JOB NO	ITEM NO	ITEM TYPE	SUBJECT	etc
	1			

JOB VALUE [   ]   No of Items [   ]

CALCULATED AUTOMATICALLY

5. Report design

The format of all the reports will be similar. The layout of the rptBusinessCustomer report is shown below:

It would be better to show a hand-drawn design for a proposed report. It is not necessary to use squared paper and lay out every character; simply show what headings you will use, what data will appear and in approximately what position.

			A.B Frames Ltd Customer Database
	Business Customer Report		
ID	Name	Address	Home Telephone
			Work Telephone
16	Mr D Grieves	19 Church St	567890
		Ipswich	453210
		Suffolk	
		IP7 5GF	
576	Mrs P Mason	34 Kipling St	745221
		Ipswich	01728-998766
		Suffolk	
		IP6 4ER	

6. Mail merge

The Mail Merge option will allow the user to load up Word directly from Access, and specify which of several queries is to be used as the source of the data. The user is given the option to use an existing letter or create a new letter. This feature is not to be totally automated as the users wish to have the flexibility to create new letters themselves, and possibly even to create new queries when they become more confident in the use of the system.

When Mail Merge is selected on the menu, instructions on how to proceed will appear on screen.

Emphasise user involvement throughout.

After discussion with the user it was decided not to produce mailing labels, as there was less work involved in using window envelopes.

In order to keep a record of which customers have been mailed and when, reports have been designed using the same queries as those used in the mail merge, so that a list can be printed out and filed after performing a mail merge.

7. Queries

Queries which pick out various categories of customer will be created and saved, as follows:

qryArtistName	Allows user to specify an artist's name, then selects all customers who have purchased a painting by that artist
qryBusinessCustomer	Selects all Business Customers
qryExhibitionCustomer	Selects all customers who have attended exhibitions
qryFramingCustomer	Selects all customers who have had a framing job done
qryJobValue	Allows user to specify a currency amount and then selects all customers who have had total jobs exceeding that amount
qryRestorationCustomer	Selects all customers who have had restoration work done
qrySalesCustomer	Selects all customers who have bought paintings etc.
qrySubjectMatter	Allows user to type in a specific subject matter and selects all customers who have had jobs specifying that subject matter
qryTapestryCustomer	Selects all customers who have had work done on Tapestries

8. Menu design

The menu structure is as follows:

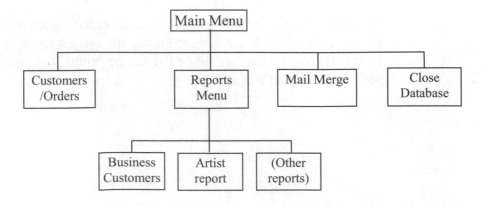

9. Systems flowchart

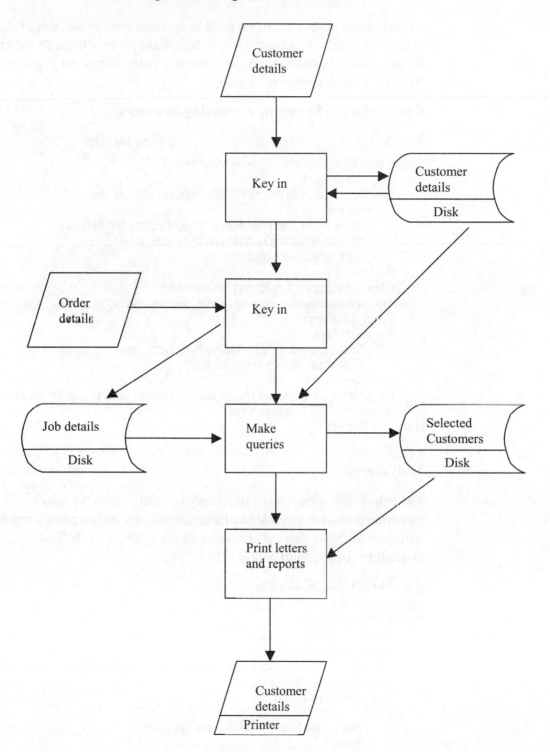

10. Module design

Visual Basic modules will be used to automate many aspects of data entry and updating of customer records. Complete listings of the code for all buttons, events etc. in the two data entry forms are given in the Systems Maintenance Section.

Entering a job for a new or existing customer

The design is expressed in the following pseudocode.

```
Select Add Customer/Order from Main Menu
For each Job Sheet:
      Use Find button to check if customer already on file
      If not found,
            Click Add Customer button to add customer details
            New CustomerID displayed in empty form
            Add customer details
      Endif
      Click Add Job button to add job details
      frmJobSheet opens with customer details displayed
      Enter job details
      For each item:
            Enter Item details including Item type, cost
            Customer record updated automatically
      Next item
      Click Job total cost and No. of items in job to update automatically
      Return to frmCustomer form
Next Job Sheet
```

Mail merge

The other main function of the database is to be able to select customers matching certain criteria and either view or print a report listing them, send them a new or existing letter, or both. The procedure for the Mail Merge will be:

```
Select Mail Merge from Main Menu
(On-screen instructions appear)
Follow instructions to
      Open database window
      Select appropriate query
      Select Office Links tool from Toolbar and select the Mail Merge option
      (Word opens automatically)
      If new letter required
      Then
            Write new letter, inserting merge fields
            Save letter
      Else
            Open existing letter
            Make any modifications required
      Endif
```

Select Tools, Mail Merge from menu to perform the Mail Merge
Close Word to return to Access
Select Reports from Main Menu
Print report to have hard copy listing of which customers mailed

Show how the design is influenced by the user's requirements or level of I.T. skills

Although it would be possible for the system to incorporate a basic letter corresponding to each query (for a particular selection of customers) the user opted to have a less automated mail merge as the situation will inevitably arise when they want to make a new query and create a new letter. This will be much easier for them if they have already got used to the procedure for performing a mail merge from scratch.

11. Security

A password will be attached to the database so that it is only accessible to someone who knows the password. Different access levels are not needed as Mr and Mrs Daniels are the only people who will be using the database.

12. Test strategy

You must describe an appropriate test strategy in the Design section. Put the detailed test plan and test results in the Testing section.

The test strategy will include five different types of testing as described below.

Logical testing

This will be used to test every aspect of each form, report and query as soon as it is implemented, using valid, invalid and extreme data. Test data will be added to test each code module and results compared with the expected results. Sufficient data will be added to ensure that there is at least one customer in each category (e.g. 'Tapestry Customer'). The test data that will be added initially is shown in Appendix 1. Subsequent tests will often involve adding new data which will then be deleted when the test works satisfactorily.

Functional testing

Each menu item will be tested in turn to ensure that no function has been missed out.

System testing

When the system is complete, the whole range of tests will be carried out again to ensure that no errors have been introduced.

Recovery testing

The computer will be re-booted while the database is open to ensure that data is not lost or corrupted in the event of a power failure.

Acceptance testing

The user will then be involved and asked to test all the capabilities of the program to ensure that all required functions are present and working in the manner expected. This testing may result in further refinements.

Assessment

The choice of Access to implement the system has been satisfactorily justified, both on the grounds that this is a package the users have already purchased and would like to use, and on the grounds that it is very suitable for this system and has all the required facilities.

The database has been correctly normalised, with three entities defined and the correct relationships between them specified. The data to be held has been suitably defined, with validations, default values and data entry shortcuts such as combo boxes, automatic conversion to uppercase etc. specified. There appears to be a weakness in that a job with ID 0 can inadvertently be added if the user chooses to return to the frmCustomer form without entering a job.

The user interface design and the method of data entry have been carefully designed to overcome the problem of not being able to locate past jobs for a customer. Visual Basic modules have been used to update automatically details on a customer according to the type and value of items on the job sheet. The Mail Merge has not been totally automated but a reasonable justification has been given for the approach taken.

The report layout for Business customers looks neat and shows the required information.

The discussion on security is brief but satisfactory for this particular system.

The test strategy is well described and backed up by a comprehensive test plan shown in the Testing section.

Mark: Performance Level 4: 10 out of 12. (Design well fitted to the situation and incorporating all the required aspects to support the development of a fully working system.)

Section 3 - Testing

1. *Test plan*

Test No.	Test	Expected result
1	Test password	Only "ABF" accepted. Main menu opens automatically.
2	Test Main menu option Customer/Orders	frmCustomer form opens
3	Enter first customer	Automatically given CustomerID 1. Default values correctly inserted
4	Enter customers 2 to 15	CustomerID incremented automatically, but can be changed by the user if required Initials and Post code capitalised automatically. Business name skipped if not business customer Tab order correct throughout form
5	Use Find Customer button to find Belles	Belles P located and displayed
6	Use the Next button to find next customer named Belles	Belles FR located and displayed
7	Press Next button again	Text on button changes to 'No More'
8	Press Add Customer, then Add Job before entering customer name	Customised error message appears: 'Enter customer details before entering job'. Customer form remains open.
9	Press Add Customer, enter customer name, then press Add Job button	frmJobSheet opens with customer name displayed. Job can be entered.
10	Press 'Return to Customer Details'	Customer form opens showing the same customer and in the subform, the job that was just added.

Test No.	Test	Expected result
11	For customer 23 (Zelter) Add Job 31, 1 item, type 'Restoration'	'Restoration' category automatically checked on frmCustomer, Job appears in subform.
12	For customer 23 Add Job 33, 1 item, type 'Framing'	'Framing' category automatically checked on frmCustomer, Job appears in subform.
13	For customer 23 Add Job 34, 1 item, type 'Tapestry'	'Tapestry' category automatically checked on frmCustomer, Job appears in subform.
14	For customer 23 Add Job 35, 1 item, type 'Exhibition'	'Exhibition' category automatically checked on frmCustomer, Job appears in subform.
15	For customer 23 Add Job 36, 1 item, type 'Sales'	'Sales' category automatically checked on frmCustomer, Job appears in subform.
16	For customer 2, add job 17 with 2 items Framing (£50) and Sales (£75), total value £125	Job total and Number of items correctly calculated, frmCustomer form correctly refreshed
17	Add Job 777 for Customer 1 (L.P. Heathcote), date 2/3/00 to test 'millennium bug'	Date recorded as 02/03/2000
18	Attempt to add another job 777	Error message: JobNo must be unique
19	Attempt to leave Job form without entering a job for Customer 1	JobNo 0 is saved on file
20	Repeat previous test	Error message: Duplicate JobNo (because 2 jobs with ID 0)
21	In frmCustomer form locate Customer 1 and highlight and delete JobNo 0	Job deleted
22	Double-click JobNo 777 in frmCustomer form with Customer 1 (L.P.Heathcote) on screen	frmJobSheet form opens with details on screen

Test No.	Test	Expected result
23	Change Item 2 price from £0 to £20, and click in Total Price field	Total job price updated on Job Form and on frmCustomer form
24	Print report of all business customers	All business customers appear on report
25	Print rptArtist report, entering artist 'Constable' for artist name	All customers who have bought a work by Constable should appear on report
26	Print rptArtist report, entering artist 'Reynolds' for whom there are no jobs	Message displayed saying that there are no customers fitting this category
27	Print rptJobValue report, specifying job value of £50	All customers with over £50 in jobs appear on report
28	Select Mail merge option	Mail merge instructions appear
29	Test Mail Merge for Exhibition customers, creating a new letter, by following Mail Merge instructions	Letters to L.P.Heathcote, Hallett, Thomas and Williams
30	Test Mail Merge for Customers whose jobs total over £1000, using existing letter	Letters to L.P.Heathcote and O.H.Head
31	Test Reports Menu option, then each submenu option	Reports correctly printed
32	Test Return to Main Menu button on frmCustomer form	Main Menu appears
33	Select Close Database	Access closes down
34	Test 'recovery' after power failure	Only current changes lost

About 30 tests should be sufficient; don't go overboard in a project with a limit on the recommended size.

2. Test results

You can include test results in an Appendix. It is not necessary to put them into a word-processed document. Use hand annotation and highlighter pen to draw the reader's attention to the important points in the screenshot.

The test results for the final test run are shown below. Errors which came to light during earlier test runs were corrected and all tests gave expected results.

Test 1: test password

When the correct password was entered, the database opened. Otherwise, the following message was displayed:

Test 2. Enter first customer in empty database

CustomerID correctly set to 1

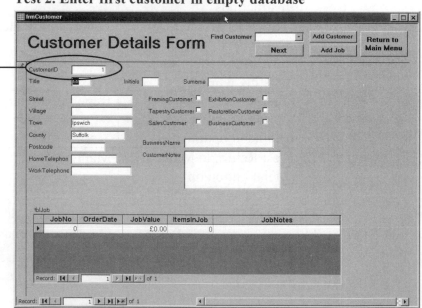

Test 3: Enter customers 2 to 15

Customer details entered. All different options, defaults and fields were tested during data entry. The tests resulted in some minor changes to field order, tab order, and default values to make data entry as smooth as possible. During user testing, the addition of a 'Delete Customer' button was discussed but rejected as the user is quite at ease with using the built-in Access 'Delete' button on the toolbar.

Test 4: Use Find Customer button to find Belles

Record for 'Belles' is displayed when selected in combo box

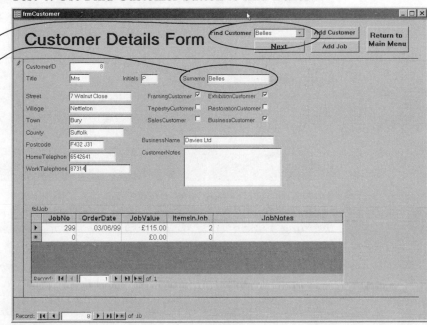

Test 8: Attempt to add job before entering customer details

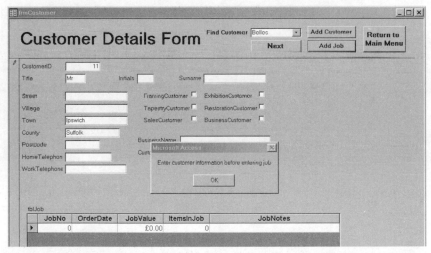

Comment: This test initially resulted in the frmJobSheet form opening with no customer details displayed, which would have left a job on the file for an unknown customer if the user had not noticed that they had forgotten to enter at least the customer's name. The message appears if the surname field is left empty when Add Job is pressed.

Test 9: Add customer name only, and then press Add Job

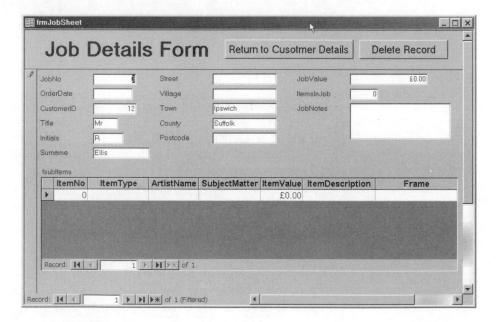

*Comment: This was an unexpected result: the customer details had not been saved by Access prior to opening the Job Sheet. The problem was fixed by inserting a line of code **Me.Refresh** in the module attached to the 'Add Job' button on the customer sheet.*

The test was repeated and worked satisfactorily as shown below.

In cases where it is difficult to show evidence that the test worked correctly, you could ask your teacher/lecturer to perform the test and sign it off.

Test 10: Press 'Return to Customer' button

Comment: Initially this had the effect of returning to the frmCustomer form but always showing Record number 1 instead of the customer for whom the job was added. The reason for this was that the Requery command was used unnecessarily on the After Update event property of the frmJobSheet form. (See systems documentation)

The code was removed and the test worked satisfactorily.

Teacher's signature:

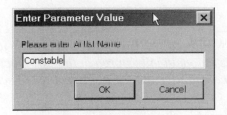

Test 25: Print rptArtist report

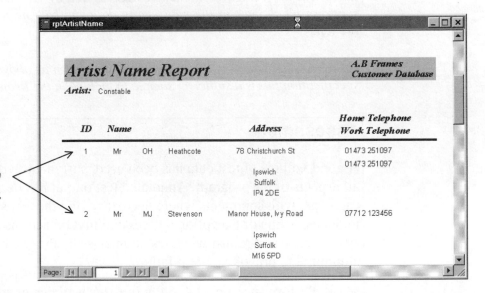

These are the only two customers who have bought works by Constable

Test 29: Mail Merge for Exhibition Customers

This output would look more authentic if it was NOT pasted into a word-processed document. Aim at authenticity rather than neatness in your evidence of testing.

Mrs C A Hallet
St Helens Street
Ipswich
Suffolk FG4 UY7

Dear Mrs Hallet

We have pleasure in inviting you to the Private View of an exhibition of recent East Anglian landscapes in watercolour from the studio of the well known artist ***Michael Nolan*** at the A.B.Frames Gallery on Thursday 21st August 1997.

Etc etc

Comments on test results can be added by hand. You should also comment on significant test results in the Systems Maintenance section.

Comment: The test allowed the user to create a new letter for Exhibition customers, which is automatically stored in the 'My Documents' folder. This is convenient for the end user but for test purposes at school/college had to be changed.

There was no 'village' in the above address and by selecting the option to suppress blank lines in the mail merge dialogue box, no unsightly spaces are left.

(In the project write-up, other tests could be shown as above. For the AQA specification this is a sufficient sample to include in the Project report)

Assessment

A good volume of test data has been used, sufficient to demonstrate all aspects of the program. Annotated test output has been shown for each test, with comments where necessary, and the test strategy includes testing of exceptional cases and invalid actions and data. The system appeared robust when tested in class by the teacher, who attempted to provoke system failure.

Mark: Performance Level 4: 5 out of 6. (A well designed test plan showing expected results supported by selected samples of carefully annotated and cross-references hard copy showing test runs that proves the reliability and robustness of the candidates system. All significant aspects thoroughly tested using extreme and/or erroneous data.)

Section 4 - System Maintenance

1. *System overview*

This Customer Information system is designed to keep records of customer profiles and their past orders. It is designed to run alongside the current manual system of recording orders, rather than replacing it. The computer will be in the shop and the owner can use it to check whether a customer who comes in is already on the database, or to check on past orders.

New data will be added to the database at a convenient time, possibly at the end of the week. The procedure that the user will follow is described in the Design Section.

2. *Tables and Relationships*

Tables and relationships were set up as specified in the Design Section. An extra table tblItemType was set up to be used as the source for the Item Type list box in the fsubItems subform of frmJobSheet. It has only one field, specifying different types of item such as Framing, Tapestry etc.

3. *Forms*

The menu structure was set up as specified in the Design Section. Forms were used as follows:

1. AB Main Menu (see user manual for screenshot)

This is specified as the startup form (using Tools, Startup) and loads automatically when the database is opened.

All buttons either opening other forms or reports, or quitting the database, were placed using wizards.

Macros/Modules used:

On Open event uses a custom-made macro named Maximise, which maximises the form.

2. AB Reports Menu (see User Manual for screenshot)

All buttons placed using wizards. Maximise macro runs on opening form.

3. Input forms (see User Manual for screenshots)

Draw the readers attention to code given in an Appendix.

> **All buttons and many fields have code modules attached. Listings are shown in Appendix 2.**

There is no need to repeat pseudocode given in the Design section, but you could refer the reader to it.

The frmCustomer form has a combo box (FindIt) displaying customer surnames so that the user can look up the record for any customer. The record source for this box is a query as follows:

SELECT DISTINCT [tblCustomer].Surname
FROM [tblCustomer]
WHERE ((([tblCustomer].Surname) Is Not Null))
ORDER BY [tblCustomer].Surname;

When a surname is selected, a macro named FindCustomer is executed to find and display the first record with the selected surname.

4. MailMergeHelp form (see user manual for screenshot)

There are no modules attached to this form.

3. Queries

Queries for reports are as listed in the Design Section. The other query named **qryCustomerJob** is used as the source for the frmJobShcct form, and combines all the Job sheet fields with the name and address fields for the customer so that these can be displayed on the frmJobSheet form.

4. Reports

These are as described in the User manual. All reports were created using wizards and then tailored to produce a more appropriate layout.

5. Mail merge letters

A sample letter named Exhibition letter was created and placed in the My Documents folder, which is the default folder for Word documents in Windows 98. The user may choose to save new letters in a different folder.

6. Macros and general modules

All listings are shown in Appendix 2.

Module name: basMisc.

(General Declarations)

Purpose: To declare two global variables used in the frmCustomer form and frmJobSheet forms.

(Function IsOpen)

Purpose: To check whether a form is open. The function uses the Visual Basic SysCmd function, which returns the state of a specified database object to indicate whether the object is open, a new object, or has been changed but not saved.

Module name: Maximise

Purpose: To maximise all forms on opening

7. Discussion of test results

You can print out the test data that you use directly from Access, either by creating a special report or by printing the tables. Do this regularly as you add new tests, so that you can easily see what output to expect from various queries and reports.

Two extra reports named rptCustomerTestData and rptJobsTestData were generated using wizards to give a hard copy of all test data used during testing. This greatly simplified the process of determining the expected output for many of the tests, and what data to use for new tests when new modules were added. The two reports are printed in Appendix 1.

The tests threw up several minor errors which have been corrected. The following points were noted:

- if the user enters a JobNo that already exists, he/she is not informed of the error until an attempt is made to leave the form, either to enter the fsubItems subform, delete the record or return to the Customer form. Solution: display a message on leaving the field.

- if the user has inadvertently left 0 in the JobNo field and then attempts to return to the frmCustomer form, a Job with ID 0 will be saved the first time. The second time, a 'Duplicate ID' error message will be displayed. The user will have to enter a different ID and then delete the record. Solution: As above; display a message on leaving field, ('JobNo must be entered')

- If Word is already open when the user starts the Mail Merge from Access, a second version of Word is automatically opened, which could cause 'Out of Memory' problems. Solution: Educate the user to close Word first, or perform the Mail Merge directly from Word.

The complete system occupied over 7 Mb of hard disk space. In order to transfer it to the user's machine it was zipped onto 2 floppy disks. The following problems arose on the user's PC:

- The screen was an older model, of lower resolution, which meant that some of the text on the forms did not fit on the screen. The forms were adjusted for the user's screen.

- The procedure for splitting the database into separate files for Data and Application (using Tools, Add-ins, Database Splitter) resulted in a message 'Not available' so this could not be done. This means that when a backup is done, the application as well as the data has to be backed up. It also means that it is not possible to hold on the owner's machine, a separate file of test data for use in the event of any problems arising.

Assessment

The system overview gives a clear overall picture of the methods used in the application. There has been extensive use of Visual Basic to tailor the system to the user's requirements and the listings are adequately documented to enable another programmer to make modifications if required. All the objects used in the database have been described.

Significant test results have been discussed satisfactorily.

Mark: Performance Level 4: 5 out of 6. (A clearly set out overall system design supported by dctails of the component parts and underlying structures. Features used describes and "design views" of the candidate's own tailoring supplied. Details of data structures and links together with samples of candidate's tailored features and macro listings self documenting or with clear annotation.)

Section 5 - User Documentation

See separate section at the end of the Project documentation.

Assessment

The user manual is well presented, with screenshots to help the user, and all aspects of the program including backup are carefully explained.

Mark: Performance Level 4: 5 out of 6. (Well presented documentation encorporating an introduction to the system describing functionality together with information on how to use the candidates system supported by samples of screen displays and error messages. The manual should be at a level appropriate for the prospective user.)

Section 6 - Appraisal

Relate your appraisal to the objectives listed in the Analysis section.

Note that the AQA only allocates 5% of the total marks to the Appraisal, whereas other Boards may allocate up to 20% to this section.

The system has been completed and installed on the user's PC. It was completed in the manner originally designed and agreed with the user, and is straightforward to use.

Referring to the original objectives listed in the Analysis section:

1. It takes only a few seconds to establish whether a customer is on file with the 50 or so records on file at the moment.

2. It is easy to go from the frmCustomer form to the frmJobSheet form using a command button, and details are automatically displayed in the Job Sheet.

3. Mrs Daniels had some problems initially with data entry, confusing Jobs and Items, as this aspect works a little differently from the manual system. However she has now entered data for over 100 customers and has no problems to report.

   Particular attention has been paid to default values, tab order, automatic capitalisation of Initials and Post Code. One problem which has come to light is that only 4 characters were allowed for

'Title', and sometimes Mrs Daniels would like to enter 'Mr and Mrs'. This can easily be adjusted.

4. All jobs for a particular customer are displayed in a subform, so it is a matter of a few seconds to double-click on a particular job to bring up the details. However, the system does not allow the user to easily look up a job from the job number (JobNo); a job can only be located by first looking up the customer, and then double-clicking the job number in the subform. It would be a good idea to add this look-up facility to the frmJobSheet form, and it would be quite simple to add a button to do so.

5. Multi-item jobs are provided for by using a subform in the frmJobSheet form.

6. All reports are implemented as specified.

7. The user has found the mail merge quite complex to perform, and in retrospect it may have been a good idea to set up sample letters to match each data source query, as it would then be possible to automate this aspect of the program more fully. However some of the problems are more to do with the user's unfamiliarity with the process of changing folders in Windows 98, and remembering where letters have been stored, than with weaknesses in the customer database.

8. See 7 above. When Mrs Daniels has completed the data entry of existing customers, I plan to go over with her the steps involved in writing a new letter and performing the mail merge, using her computer.

9. The menus work as planned.

You should ask the user to write you a letter realistically evaluating the strengths and weaknesses of your system from their point of view. This MUST be authentic to be of any value.

Some other minor problems have been noted in the 'Discussion of Test Results' in the Systems Maintenance section.

The next stage in computerisation could very well be to integrate this database with an Accounts system, since all orders are stored together with the order values.

The AQA mark scheme specifies the inclusion of 'analysis of feedback from users' for full marks in this section.

Assessment

Mark: Performance Level 3: 2 out of 3. (Achievement clearly and directly related to objectives.Analysis of any improvements needed together with realistic suggestions of how these could be incorporated. Analysis of feedback from users.)

Assessment of Technical Solution

(The user manual gives a good picture of how the final system works, but the assessor will need to see a demonstration to assess the implementation, and will note down any good and bad points on the assessment sheet which is sent to the moderator.)

The two data entry forms have been carefully tailored to the user's requirements, with Visual Basic code behind many of the fields to automate or validate data entry where possible. Individual customers can quickly be located using the Find Customer button and all a customer's past jobs are summarised in a subform. Details of a job can be accessed by double-clicking the appropriate job number.

The Mail Merge, which is an important part of the user's requirements (as a means of keeping in touch with customers) is only partially automated, with the user following instructions to automatically load Word and either create a new letter or use an existing one, selecting the appropriate data source and inserting the merge fields.

Testing by the class teacher revealed no errors and only one or two minor weaknesses (e.g. Item number defaults to 1 but could automatically increment to 2, 3 etc. for subsequent items for the same job.) All parts of the system were easy and convenient to use.

Mark: Performance Level 4: 10 out of 12 (A robust fully working project that demonstrates a high standard of technical competence over a range of complex tasks. Use of appropriate macro-programming language to provide a solution fully fitted to the user requirements.)

This report is approximately 6000 words, excluding user manual, test data and module listings. This is the recommended limit for an AEB A Level project.

Assessment of Quality of Communication

In general the report is well written with no obvious mistakes of spelling or grammar.

Mark: Performance Level 1: 3 out of 3. (Clearly and logically presented. Grammar, punctuation and spelling of an acceptable standard with few and minor errors.)

Overall grade

Overall grade for this project:

Analysis	10	out of	12
Design	10	out of	12
Technical solution	10	out of	12
System Testing	5	out of	6
System Maintenance	5	out of	6
User Manual	5	out of	6
Appraisal	2	out of	3
Quality of Language	3	out of	3

Total   50 out of 60 = 83% (Grade A)

A.B.Frames

Customer Database

User Manual

User Manual

*Your user manual
should contain a
separate table of
contents*

Table of Contents

Introduction 39

Initial Set-up 39

Menu options 39

Entering Customers and Jobs 40

Looking up Customer Details 42

Reports 43

Printing a report 45

Mail Merge 45

Backing Up the System 48

Restoring from Backup Disks 49

*Start with an introduction so the user knows immediately what the system is all about. Remember that for the AQA specification it is sufficient to show a **sample** of each section of the user manual. It should not be more than 4 or 5 pages including screen shots.*

Introduction

This Customer Information system is designed to help you with two main tasks:

- keep track of all customer jobs so that you can easily look up a past job if required, or find out who your best customers are

- keep track of all your customers and their major interests, such as particular artists or subjects, having tapestries framed, etc. so that you can send letters to carefully selected customers informing them of exhibitions, special offers and so on.

The system has been designed in Access 2000 running under Windows 95. You will need a PC with at least 16Mb of memory, and 12Mb of free space on your hard disk to use the system effectively.

Initial Set-up

Passwords

To remove or change the current password required to enter the database, you must choose *Unset Database Password* from the *Tools > Security* menu at the top of the screen. If you then wish to add a new password, go again to the *Tools* menu and the option should now have changed to *Set Database Password*. Select this option, and then type in and verify the new password when asked. **Note: the password is case sensitive, e.g. if the password is "AB", it will not allow access if you type in "ab".**

Menu options

The Main Menu will automatically appear when you open the database.

Include screenshots of all the important screens

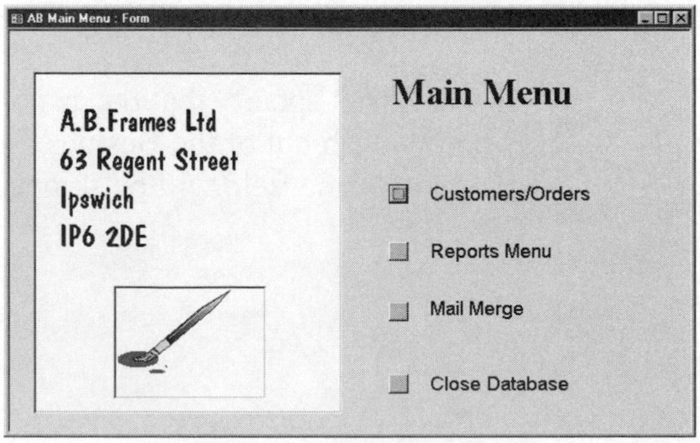

Figure 1: The main menu

Entering Customers and Jobs

Adding a Customer

To enter a new customer you select Customers/Orders from the Main Menu to open the frmCustomer form. Click the *Add Customer* Button, and the *CustomerID* will automatically increment its value. You can then enter all other details.

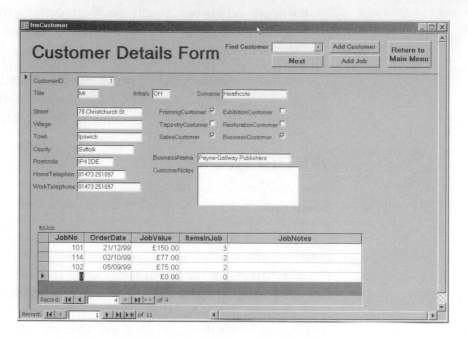

Figure 2: The frmCustomer form

Notes on the frmCustomer Form:

Give the user guidance on data entry where necessary

- Ipswich is the default town, and Suffolk the default County but you can of course change these entries

- If you enter Customer Initials or Postcode in lower case letters, they will automatically change to upper case on leaving the field

- If you do not specify that the customer is a business customer, when you tab out of the BusinessCustomer (Yes/No) field the BusinessName field will be skipped.

Adding a job

In order to add a job for a customer you must first have that customer's details up on the frmCustomer form (this will already be the case if you have just entered the customer). You can find any customer's record by clicking the arrow in the *Find Customer* box at the top of the form, and selecting the surname of the customer you are looking for. Alternatively you can type in the surname you are looking for in the box. If the details that appear have the correct surname but it is not the correct customer, clicking the *Next* button will take you to the next customer with that surname.

When you have the correct details on screen, select the *Add Job* button. This will take you to the Job Details form, and the CustomerID, name and address should automatically appear in the top right of the form. You can then enter the *Job No* and *Order date*, followed by the rest of the Job Details.

When this is complete, return to the frmCustomer form by clicking the *Return to frmCustomer form* button at the top right of the form. On return to the frmCustomer form you will see that the Job details you have just entered are in the box at the bottom of the form, along with all other previous jobs.

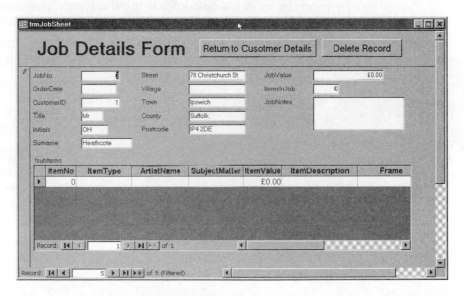

Figure 3: The Job Details form

Notes on the Job Details form

• After entering the items, when you tab into the Job Value and Items In Job fields, they will be automatically calculated and displayed.

- You should not leave JobNo as 0, even if you change your mind about entering a new job for this customer. Instead, press the Delete Record button, which will make the JobNo field blank, and it will then be safe to exit the form.

Changing Job Details

In order to change details of a job, you must have the relevant customer's details up on the frmCustomer form. Find the job in the box at the bottom of the form, and double-click on the *Job No* of the job you wish to change, and this will take you to the Job Details form.

If you want to delete the job altogether, you can do this in the frmCustomer form by simply highlighting the row which contains the job you wish to delete, and pressing *Delete* on the keyboard. Deleting can also be done using the *Delete* button on the Job Details Form.

Looking up Customer Details

Looking up previous jobs for a customer

Find the relevant customer using the *Find Customer* box, and the *Next* button. You can then see the summary of each job the customer has had done in the box at the bottom of the screen. In order to see the full job details, double-click on the *Job No* of the job you want to see, and this will take you to the Job Details form.

Reports

When you select **Reports Menu** from the main menu, a second menu appears:

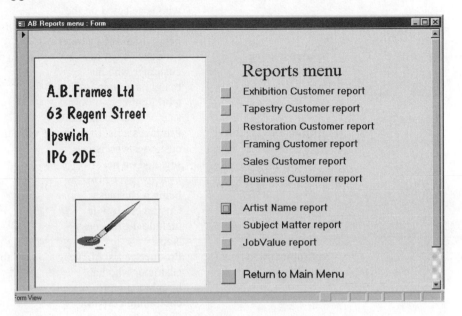

Figure 4: The Reports menu

Summary of Each Report

Report Name	What It Does	Query it is Based on
rptExhibitionCustomer	Produces a list of every customer who has bought something at an exhibition, or is selected on the *frmCustomer Form* as being an exhibition Customer.	qryExhibitionCustomer
rptTapestryCustomer	Produces a list of every customer who has had a tapestry framed, or who is selected on the *frmCustomer Form* as being a Tapestry Customer	qryTapestryCustomer
rptRestorationCustomer	Produces a list of every customer who has had something restored or who is selected on the *frmCustomer Form* as being a restoration Customer	qryRestorationCustomer
rptFramingCustomer	Produces a list of every customer who has had something framed, or	qryFramingCustomer

	who is selected on the frmCustomer form as being a framing Customer	
rptSalesCustomer	Produces a list of every customer who has bought something, or who is selected on the frmCustomer form as being a Sales Customer	qrySalesCustomer
rptArtistName	Produces a list of every customer who has bought a certain artist's work, either as a normal sale or in an exhibition	qryArtistName
rptBusinessCustomer	Produces a list of every customer who is selected on the *frmCustomer Form* as being a Business Customer. It will include the business Names	qryBusinessCustomer
rptSubjectMatter	Produces a list of every customer who has bought a picture containing certain Subject Matter	qrySubjectMatter
rptJobValue	Produces a list of every customer who has spent more than the amount you type in	qryJobValue

Viewing a report on screen

In the Reports Menu, click the report you want to view. If the report requires information, a dialogue box will appear asking you to type in a word or value. The report will then appear on screen for you to view. If the report is more than one page long, you can get to the other pages by using the navigation buttons at the bottom of the screen as shown below:

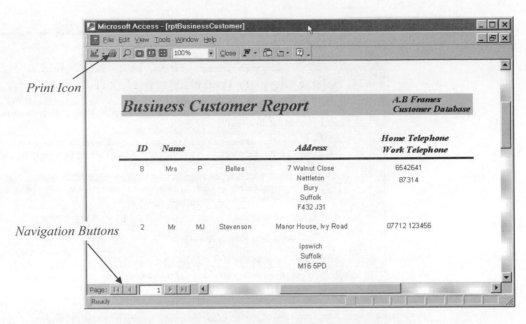

Figure 5: Viewing a report before printing it

Printing a report

To print a report you first view it on screen as above, then click the print icon at the top of the screen, shown above.

Mail Merge

For each query that you will want to use as the basis of a mail merge you will need a different merge letter, which you will create yourself as the need arises, and save in the My Documents folder using a meaningful name (e.g. **Sales letter Sep 99.doc** for a letter sent to all Sales customers in September 1999).

To perform a mail merge, you can select the Mail Merge option from the main menu to bring up further instructions, as shown below. Once you get used to the process, you can skip the menu option and open the database window directly.

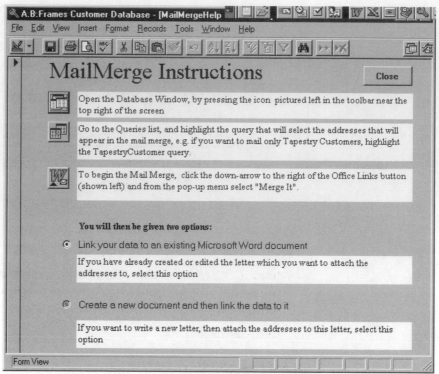

Figure 6: Instructions for the Mail Merge

The steps in the Mail Merge are as follows:

1. From the database window, click the Queries tab and click qryBusinessCustomer to select it. This will bc thc source of names and addresses for the mail merge.

2. Press the down arrow to the right of the OfficeLinks tool. Select Merge it from the pop-up menu.

OfficeLinks tool

3. The Microsoft Word Mail Merge Wizard dialogue box opens. If you want to create a new letter, select the second option: Create a new document and then link the data to it.

4. Word opens ready to create the standard letter. Press Enter about 6 times to leave some space at the top of the letter for a standard letterhead, inserting the date, etc.

5. Click the Insert Merge Field in the menu bar. The field list is displayed.

Figure 7: Inserting merge fields

6. Click Title. The field <<Title>> is placed in your letter. Place
    the other fields for name and address, leaving spaces and
    pressing Enter for each new line. The actual text of the letter
    will be altered by the user. Your letter should appear something
    like Figure 8.

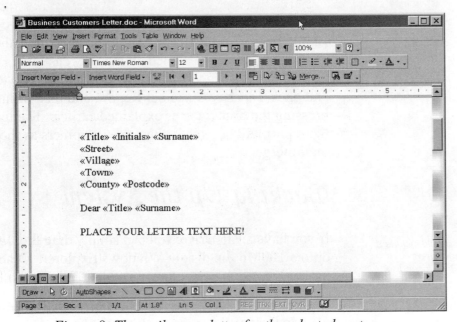

Figure 8: The mail merge letter for the selected customers

7. Select Tools, Mail Merge and click Step 3: Merge.

8. In the next dialogue box, click Merge.

9. A letter appears for each selected customer, which can be
    printed.

10. Close without saving - you do not need to keep the letters,
    which are distinct from the master letter where the merge fields

were placed. Save this document as "Business Customers Letter" or some other suitable title, in a convenient folder e.g. My Documents.

If you have a merge letter for the query you wish to use, open up that letter so you have it on screen, and make any changes you wish to it, such as changing the date, and the main letter. The merge fields should not need to be changed.

1. Go to Tools, Mail Merge, then Option 3: Merge. Select Merge from the next menu.

2. Go to File, Print, Current Page to check the letters.

3. If the letter is satisfactory, print all the letters by going to File, Print, All.

4. Close the actual merge document without saving. Access will have given it a name such as Form Letters1.

Keeping a record of who was mailed

If you would like to keep a record of who you have mailed, you should print a report straight after you have done the mail merge. For example, if you have mailed all tapestry customers using a merge based on the qryTapestryCustomer query, then go to the reports menu and click Tapestry Customer Report, and then print the report by pressing the print icon as explained earlier. The list of customers on the report will be exactly the same customers as those who are in the mail merge.

Backing Up the System

You should include a paragraph on backup procedures

If you have a Zip Drive, you can simply drag the *Abframe.mdb* file onto a 100Mb Zip disk in Windows Explorer. Otherwise the file will probably need to be compressed, using WinZip, to fit onto a diskette.

If you are backing up for the first time, have 2 formatted 1.4Mb diskettes, labelled #1, #2;

1. Close the database application.

2. Open Windows Explorer and insert disk #1.

3. In the *C:\ABDB* folder find the file *Abframe.mdb* and right mouse click on it.

4. On the popup menu that appears, choose **Add to Zip**.

5. In the 'Add to Archive' box, change the line to *A:\Abframe.zip* and click **Add**. Confirm **Yes** if prompted to overwrite the existing file. If the system requests a second disk, insert disk #2.

6. Close the WinZip window.

Restoring from Backup Disks

If you lose data for any reason and need to restore the database from your backup disks, follow the following steps:

1. Insert the backup disk.

You can also include your name and telephone number as the 'Help-line number' to contact in the event of any problems arising.

2. If the file is *Abframe.zip*, right-click on it, choose **Extract to...** from the menu.

3. In the 'Extract To' box enter *C:\ABDB* and click **Extract**.

4. Confirm **Yes** if prompted to overwrite the existing file. If the system requests a second disk, insert disk #2.

Appendix 1

Test Data

CUSTOMER DETAILS

ID	Title	Surname	Init	Street	Town	County	Postcode	Sales	Framing	Rest	Tapestry	Exhib	Bus	BusinessNum
1	Mr	Heathcote	L P	11 Bullen	Ipswich	Suffol	IP8 4JD	☑	☑	☐	☐	☐	☐	
2	Mrs	Head	OH	43 MacInt	Ipswich	Suffol	IP9 7HJ	☐	☑	☑	☐	☐	☑	Solos
3	Ms	James	S.J	57 Orchar	Ipswich	Suffol	IP15 9T	☐	☐	☐	☐	☐	☑	Davries Ltd
4	Mrs	Belles	P	7 Walnut	Bury	Suffol	F432 J	☐	☑	☑	☐	☐	☐	
5	Mr	Jaynes	PE	34Hervey	Sudbury	Suffol	IP8 7H	☑	☑	☑	☐	☐	☐	
6	Mr	Belles	FR	78 The St	Ipswich	Suffol	1p4 2d	☑	☑	☑	☑	☑	☐	
7	Mr	Cladon	RB	16 Chilter	Ipswich	Suffol	IP7 4W	☑	☑	☐	☐	☐	☐	
9	Mrs	Heathcote	PM	78 Christ	Ipswich	Suffol	IP4 2D	☐	☑	☐	☐	☐	☐	
10	Mr	Blair	T W	10 Downi	London		54Y 5H	☐	☐	☐	☐	☐	☐	
11	Mr	Feavyour	JA	29 Herve	Ipswich	Suffol	ER3 RT	☐	☐	☐	☐	☐	☐	
12	Mrs	Smith	A S	33 Northg	Ipswich	Suffol	GH3 T	☐	☐	☑	☑	☑	☐	
13	Mrs	Hallet	C A	St Helens	Ipswich	Suffol	FG4 U	☐	☐	☐	☐	☐	☐	
14	Mrs	Cooper	C S	99 Wimbl	Ealing	Londo	W12 6	☐	☐	☐	☐	☐	☐	
15	Ms	Thomas	P.J	56 Rosec	Ipswich	Suffol		☐	☐	☐	☐	☐	☐	
16	Mr	James	ERD	25 Roma	Colchest	Essex	CO9 7Y	☐	☐	☐	☐	☑	☐	
17	Mrs	Williams	GH	12 Eurlin	Ipswich	Suffol		☐	☑	☐	☐	☐	☐	
18	Mrs	Morgan	CT	10 St Mat	Ipswich	Suffol		☑	☑	☐	☐	☐	☐	
19	Mrs	Golding	D	13 Eullen	Ipswich	Suffol	P8 4JD	☐	☑	☐	☐	☐	☐	
20	Miss	Johns		21 Eenac	Ipswich	Suffol		☐	☑	☐	☐	☐	☐	
21	Mrs	Weeden	J	Chalet, C	Ipswich	Suffol		☐	☑	☐	☐	☐	☐	
22	Miss	Heathcote	FR	56 Withip	Ipswich	Suffol	P4 3S	☐	☑	☑	☑	☑	☑	
23	Mr	Zelter	Z	The Whit	Orford	Suffol		☐	☑	☐	☐	☐	☑	
24	Mr	Ferdinand	T		Ipswich	Suffol		☐	☐	☐	☐	☐	☑	
25	Mr	Honeycut	BJ	Back Roa	Porking	Suffol	IP4 5F	☐	☐	☐	☐	☐	☐	
26	Mr	Pierce	HK	13 High S	Little Sno	Suffol	IP7 2N	☐	☐	☐	☐	☐	☐	
27	Mrs	Donohue	K	Wisteria		Suffol	IP9 5G	☐	☐	☐	☐	☐	☐	
28	Ms	Jones	B	Hill Hous	Wutherin	Norfol	NN6 8D	☐	☐	☐	☑	☐	☑	
29	Mr	Colquhoun	L		Dublin	Eire	E19 5M	☐	☐	☐	☐	☐	☐	
30	Cmd	Chumley	S	Moby Do		Suffol	IP7 3K	☐	☐	☐	☐	☐	☑	
31	Mr	Honeycut	WW	Tide Mill	Woodbrid	Suffol	IP23 6	☐	☐	☐	☐	☐	☑	
32	Col	Carruthers	JP	Alamein	Aldershot	Hants	HA3 9H	☐	☐	☐	☐	☐	☑	

JOBS

JobNo	ItemNo	ItemType	ArtistName	SubjectMatter	ItemValue	CustomerID	OrderDate
4	1	Sales	Constable		£150.00	2	23/05/97
17	1	Framing			£50.00	2	12/05/97
17	2	Sales	James Harvey	dogs	£75.00	2	12/05/97
31	1	Restoration			£55.00	23	
33	1	Framing			£300.00	23	
34	1	Tapestry			£760.00	23	
35	1	Exhibition			£3,000.00	2	01/01/00
36	1				£2,500.00	1	01/01/00
43	1	Framing			£17.00	24	01/09/97
45	1	Sales			£23.00	5	
76	1	Sales			£44.00	7	02/03/97
76	2	sales			£3.00	7	02/03/97
123	1	sales			£73.00	5	02/02/97
155	1	Framing	Bates	Horses	£25.00	11	01/11/97
299	1	Restoration			£55.00	4	03/09/97
299	2				£60.00	4	03/09/97
599	1	framing			£23.00	1	03/06/97
599	2	sales			£7.00	1	03/06/97
677	1	Sales			£11.00	1	01/01/97
777	1	framing			£33.00	1	02/03/00
777	2	sales	Andrew Foster	flowers	£0.00	1	02/03/00
777	3	sales	Mondrian	cubes	£0.00	1	02/03/00
778	1	Sales	Andrew Foster	dogs	£50.00	22	03/05/97
778	2	Framing		cats	£20.00	22	03/05/97
911	1	Sales	James Harvey	dogs	£50.00	12	09/07/97
3337	1	Sales		flowers	£35.00	10	03/09/97
3337	2	Framing			£25.00	10	03/09/97
3337	3	Restoration			£5.00	10	03/09/97
3337	4	Sales			£5.00	10	03/09/97
3337	5	Restoration			£10.00	10	03/09/97
5098	1	Framing			£20.10	21	01/09/95
5099	1	Framing			£48.00	20	05/09/95
5656	1	Sales	Andrew Foster	dogs	£60.00	19	05/07/97
5656	2	Framing			£40.00	19	05/07/97

Appendix 2

Module Listings

MODULE LISTINGS

1. Global Module

Name: **basMisc**

Purpose: **To declare global variables**

               To define global function IsOpen

Used in frmJobSheet and fsubItem subform

```
Option Compare Database
        Public DisplayJob As Boolean
        Public JobNum As Long
Option Explicit

Public Function IsOpen(ByVal StrFormName As String) As Boolean
' Returns true if the specified form is open in form view

Const conDesignView = 0
Const conObjStateClosed = 0
IsOpen = False
If SysCmd(acSysCmdGetObjectState, acForm, StrFormName) <>
conObjStateClosed Then
    If Forms(StrFormName).CurrentView <> conDesignView Then
        IsOpen = True
    End If
End If

End Function
```

SysCmd is a built in Visual Basic function

Annotate your listings by hand. Make clear which modules YOU wrote, and which code was created automatically by wizards.

2. frmCustomer form (see User Manual for screenshot)

All buttons and many fields have code modules attached. Listings are shown below.

```
Option Compare Database
Option Explicit

Private Sub BusinessCustomer_Exit(Cancel As Integer)
'Skip the Business Name control if not a business customer
    If BusinessCustomer = True Then
        BusinessName.SetFocus
    Else
        CustomerNotes.SetFocus
    End If
End Sub
```

```
Private Sub FindNext_Click()
'This module runs when the Find Next button is presssed.
'It finds the next customer with the same surname as the current record.
'If there are no more matching customers, the button caption changes to 'No More'

    Dim CR As String

    CR = CustomerID
    Surname.SetFocus
    DoCmd.FindRecord (Surname), , , , , , False
    FindNext.SetFocus

    If CustomerID = CR Then
        FindNext.Caption = "No more"
    End If
End Sub
```

Must set the parameter to False otherwise it gets stuck on current record

```
Private Sub FindNext_LostFocus()
    FindNext.Caption = "Next"
End Sub

Private Sub Form_Current()
'This ensures that the surname in the combo box matches the current record
    FindIt = Surname
End Sub

Sub AddCustomer_Click()
'This module runs when the Add Customer button is clicked

Dim CustID As Long                      'variable type Long Integer
On Error GoTo Err_AddCustomer_Click     'built-in error routine

    DoCmd.GoToRecord , , acLast
    CustID = CustomerID                 'save the value of CustomerID
    If CustID = 0 Then                  'allow for the very first record
        CustomerID = 1
    Else
        DoCmd.GoToRecord , , acNext     'go to a new record
        CustomerID = CustID + 1         'increment the CustomerID
    End If
    Title.SetFocus                      'move cursor to Title control

Exit_AddCustomer_Click:
    Exit Sub

Err_AddCustomer_Click:
    MsgBox Err.Description
    Resume Exit_AddCustomer_Click

End Sub
```

This module automatically assigns the next number to a new customer

```
Private Sub Initials_Exit(Cancel As Integer)
 'Change Initials to uppercase
    Initials = UCase(Initials)
End Sub


Private Sub Postcode_Exit(Cancel As Integer)
  'Change Post Code to Uppercase
    Postcode = UCase(Postcode)
End Sub


Sub AddJob_Click()
On Error GoTo Err_AddJob_Click
'Clicking the Add Job button causes this module to be run

    Dim stDocName As String
    Dim stLinkCriteria As String

    'The form must be refreshed before opening the Job sheet
    'in order to save the customer record

    Me.Refresh

    If IsNull(Me![Surname]) Then
        MsgBox "Enter customer information before entering job"
    Else
        'DisplayJob is a global variable defined in Misc
        'and tested in frmJobSheet On Open to determine what
        'event opened the frmJobSheet form, pressing the Add Job button
        'or double-clicking a JobNo in the subform.

        DisplayJob = False
        stDocName = "Job Sheet"

        stLinkCriteria = "[CustomerID]=" & Me![CustomerID]
        DoCmd.OpenForm stDocName, , , stLinkCriteria
    End If

Exit_AddJob_Click:
    Exit Sub

Err_AddJob_Click:
    MsgBox Err.Description
    Resume Exit_AddJob_Click

End Sub
```

> This code is created automatically by the wizard when you place a command to open a form

```
Sub Menu_Click()
'This runs when the Return to Main Menu button is clicked
On Error GoTo Err_Menu_Click

    Dim stDocName As String
    Dim stLinkCriteria As String

    stDocName = "AB Main Menu"
    DoCmd.OpenForm stDocName, , , stLinkCriteria

Exit_Menu_Click:
    Exit Sub

Err_Menu_Click:
    MsgBox Err.Description
    Resume Exit_Menu_Click

End Sub
```

Command button code created automatically by wizard

3.   fsubJobs (Subform)

This subform of the customer form displays a summary of all the previous jobs for the current customer. Details of any job can be obtained by double-clicking a JobNo.

The Double-click event module is shown below.

```
Private Sub JobNO_DblClick(Cancel As Integer)
'DisplayJob and JobNum are public variables declared in the module Misc.
'DisplayJob is  is set to TRUE here
'to indicate that the user has double-clicked JobNo.
'It will be tested in the Open event of the Job Sheet form.
'JobNum will also be used in the Open event of the Job Sheet form.
'to enable the correct Job Sheet to be found and displayed.

    DisplayJob = True
    JobNum = JobNo
    DoCmd.OpenForm "frmJobSheet"
End Sub
```

Current job number saved in JobNum

4. Job Sheet (see user manual for screenshot)

The Job sheet is opened directly from the frmCustomer form.
Modules attached to various events are shown below:

```
Private Sub Form_AfterUpdate()
    If IsOpen("frmCustomer") Then
    ' Requery the subform in the frmCustomer form to show new job
    '    Forms![frmCustomer].Requery

    'Note: Testing showed that this code was not necessary and caused
    'the customer form to open at the first record instead of the current record.


    Else
        MsgBox "Customer Form not open"
    End If
End Sub
```

Function IsOpen is defined in global module basMisc

```
Private Sub Form_Open(Cancel As Integer)
    If IsOpen("frmCustomer") Then
'DisplayJob is set to TRUE in the fsubJobs (Subform) of the frmCustomer form
'when a user double-clicks JobNo.
'DisplayJob is set to FALSE if the user clicks the AddJob button.
        If DisplayJob = False Then
          DoCmd.GoToRecord , , acLast
          If Not IsNull(Me![JobNo]) Then
             DoCmd.GoToRecord , , acNext
          End If
         Forms![frmJobSheet]![CustomerID] = Forms![frmCustomer]![CustomerID]

        Else
          'user wants to display a job whose number was stored in JobNum
          'in the Double-click event code in fsubJobs
          'so look for that job and display it

          JobNo.SetFocus
          DoCmd.FindRecord jobNum
        End If
      Else
        MsgBox "The Customer Details form must be open before you can enter a job"
        DoCmd.Close acForm, "frmJobSheet"
      End If
End Sub
```

```
Private Sub ItemsInJob_Enter()
    Forms![frmJobSheet]![ItemsInJob] = DCount("[ItemNo]", "tblItem",
"[JobNo]=Forms![frmJobSheet].[JobNo]")
End Sub

Private Sub JobValue_Enter()
Forms![frmJobSheet]![JobValue] = DSum("[ItemValue]", "tblItem",
"[JobNo]=Forms![frmJobSheet].[JobNo]")
End Sub


Sub ReturnToCustomer_Click()
On Error GoTo Err_ReturnToCustomer_Click

    'refresh the frmCustomer form so that it displays
    'the changes made in this form
        Forms![frmCustomer].Refresh

    DoCmd.Close
Exit_ReturnToCustomer_Click:
    Exit Sub

Err_ReturnToCustomer_Click:
    MsgBox Err.Description
    Resume Exit_ReturnToCustomer_Click

End Sub
Sub delete_Click()
On Error GoTo Err_delete_Click

    DoCmd.DoMenuItem acFormBar, acEditMenu, 8, , acMenuVer70
    DoCmd.DoMenuItem acFormBar, acEditMenu, 6, , acMenuVer70

Exit_delete_Click:
    Exit Sub

Err_delete_Click:
    MsgBox Err.Description
    Resume Exit_delete_Click

End Sub
```

These lines were added to the code generated automatically by the command button wizard

5.   fsubItems

This subform allows the user to enter several items on one job sheet. Code for the Item Type exit event module is shown below.

```
Private Sub ItemType_Exit(Cancel As Integer)

'Sets the relevant field in the tblCustomer table according to ItemType

   If IsOpen("frmCustomer") Then
      Select Case Me![ItemType]
         Case "Exhibition"
            Forms![frmCustomer]![ExhibitionCustomer] = True
         Case "Framing"
            Forms![frmCustomer]![FramingCustomer] = True
         Case "Restoration"
            Forms![frmCustomer]![RestorationCustomer] = True
         Case "Sales"
            Forms![frmCustomer]![SalesCustomer] = True
         Case "Tapestry"
            Forms![frmCustomer]![TapestryCustomer] = True
      End Select
   Else
      MsgBox "The Customer form must be open "
   End If
End Sub
```

Index

Note: Index entries apply to Part 1 only.

Access Basic 57
Appraisal 112
Assignment statement 58
Attribute 21
Autoexec macro 99
Automatic calculations 81
Boolean data type 79
Breakpoint 102
Combo Box 51, 52, 56
Command button 59
Conceptual model 21
Conditional statement 65
Creating a form with a subform 41
Criteria 95
Data validation 25
Database objects 72
DCount 81
Debug window 101
Declaring variables 65
Default values, setting 71
DoCmd 58, 65
Documentation 108
DSum 81
Enforce Referential Integrity 35
Entity 21
Entity-relationship diagram 22
Find record 55
Form with subform
    creating a 41
Function
    DCount 81
    DSum 81
    Sum 95
    SysCmd 79
    UCase 71
    writing 78
Global variables 88
Help, online 62
If...then...else 65
Immediate window 101
Interview 12
Labels, mailing 44
List Box 84
Logical testing 29
Macro
    Autoexec 99
    SetValue 58
Macros 54
Mail merge letter 45
Mailing labels 44
Menu system, creating 47
Message box 104
Method
    FindRecord 62
    Refresh 93
    SetFocus 58

Naming conventions 23
Object Browser 71, 86
Objectives
    qualitative 17
    quantitative 17
Objects
    referring to 72
Online help 62
Password 99
Print Screen 26
Programming
    macros 54
    modules 57
Prototyping 31
Query
    combining tables with 38
    creating 38
Referential Integrity 35
Refresh method 93
Relationship 22
    defining 35
Schedule 6
Security 28, 99
Select Case 85
Separator 73
SQL 54, 65
Stepping over procedures 103
Stepping through code 103
Subform 39, 41
Sum function 95
SysCmd function 79
System maintenance 111
System outline chart 21
Systems flow chart 27
Tab order, customising 69
Test
    plan 105, 106
    results 107
    strategy 28
Testing
    acceptance 30
    functional 29
    logical 29
    module 106
    recovery 29
    system 29, 106
Testing objectives 105
UCase 71
User interface 25
User manual 111
Validation 25
Variable 61, 65
    global 88
    public 89
Visual Basic for Applications 57
Wordprocessing skills 109

PROJECT TITLE: **DEVELOPED BY:**

TABLE NAME:

Attribute name	Data type	Length	Default value	Description, validation, comments

Test Plan

Test No.	Test data	Purpose	Expected result	Comment/ Verified

Successful ICT Projects in Word (2nd edition)

by P.M.Heathcote
February 2000   208pp   ISBN 1 903112 25 7

This text, updated for the 2001 syllabus and Office 2000, covers the essential features of Word from basic editing and formatting right through to advanced features such as templates, macros, customised toolbars and menus. It is suitable for students on a number of courses such as 'A' Level or Advanced VCE (GNVQ) ICT, HNC and HND in Business Information Technology and Access to HE.
It gives ideas for suitable projects and explains how to complete each phase from Analysis and Design through to Implementation, Testing and Evaluation. AQA Project Guidelines and a mark scheme are included in an Appendix.

Successful ICT Projects in Excel (2nd edition)

by P.M. Heathcote
June 2000   208pp   ISBN 1 903112 26 5

Excel is a powerful and versatile spreadsheet program which is eminently suitable for project work at every level from Advanced VCE (GNVQ) ICT to degree work. This book is also invaluable for staff development, and caters for users of Excel 2000, 97, 7 and 5.

A sample project demonstrates how to lay out a complete project report, and the AQA project mark scheme is also included. The template for the sample project as well as a sample chapter entitled 'Project Ideas' are available on the web site www.payne-gallway.co.uk

Successful ICT Projects in Access (2nd edition)

by P.M. Heathcote
July 2000   224pp   ISBN 1 903112 27 3

This book will help students to complete a project in MS Access, using version 7, 97 or 2000. It covers database design, creating tables, forms and subforms, queries, importing and exporting data to other packages, analysing and processing data, reports, macros and some Visual Basic for Applications. It includes advice on choice of projects and a sample project.

It is suitable for students on a wide range of courses such as 'A' Level or Advanced VCE (GNVQ) ICT, HNC and HND in Business Information Technology and Access to HE.

Successful ICT Projects in FrontPage

by R.S.U. Heathcote
May 2000   208pp   ISBN 1 903112 28 1

This book is designed to help students on an 'A' Level, Advanced VCE (GNVQ) or similar course to design and implement a Web site using MS FrontPage 2000. It assumes no previous knowledge of FrontPage and takes the reader from the basics such as entering, editing and formatting text and images on a Web page through to advanced features such as writing scripts, gathering data from forms, and making use of active components. A wide range of examples is used to illustrate the different facilities of FrontPage, and a sample project shows students how to tackle and document each stage of project work.

Software:

Algorithms and Data Structures (2nd Edition)

by P.M.Heathcote and E.Morgan

Published March 1st 1998. Site Licence £90.00 (plus VAT)
ISBN 0 9532490 1 8

This highly popular interactive package can be loaded and run on a network and gives students approximately 10 hours of interactive tuition on how to tackle problems involving data structures. It contains 6 units covering Programming fundamentals, Sorting and Searching, Linked Lists, Queues, Stacks and Trees. A seventh unit tests students on the concepts they have learned.

Revision Software

Content author: Alison Day   *Software: A Baillie and R Woods*

This Revision package has a completely new interface and new questions for the AQA modules written by experienced examiner Alison Day. The package is supplied on CD and may be installed on any computer in the school or college, leased on an annual basis.

Each package consists of several quizzes on different areas of the specification with up to 9 different topic areas being covered in each package. A random 10 questions from a bank of 30 or more on each topic are given each time a student attempts a quiz, and a full explanation is given after each question is attempted.

'AS' Computing Revision
ISBN 1 903112 85 0   Published March 2002   Annual Site Licence £90.00 (plus VAT)

'A2' Computing Revision
ISBN 1 903112 87 7   Published September 2002   Annual Site Licence £90.00 (plus VAT)

Hundreds of centres have already discovered the benefits of our computer-aided learning software, written especially for 'A' Level Computing students and unique in the market! The packages are straightforward to install and run, offer excellent value for money and keep students interested and motivated.

The software is supplied on CD-ROM for Windows 95, 98, NT Server or 2000, XP (but not MacOS).
Inspection copies of books and a free demo disk of both 'Algorithms and Data Structures' and
'Computing Revision' are available from our distributors:

BEBC Distribution
P.O. Box 3371
Poole, Dorset
BH12 3LL

Tel: 01202 712909   Fax: 01202 712913   E-mail: pg@bebc.co.uk